WORLD OF
GEEKCRAFT

WORLD OF GEEKCRAFT

STEP-BY-STEP INSTRUCTIONS FOR 25 SUPER-COOL CRAFT PROJECTS

BY *Susan Beal*

PHOTOGRAPHS BY Jay B Sauceda

CHRONICLE BOOKS

SAN FRANCISCO

For My Dad

Library of Congress Cataloging-in-Publication Data
Beal, Susan.
    World of geekcraft : step-by-step instructions for 25 super-cool craft projects / Susan Beal.
        p. cm.
    ISBN: 978-0-8118-7461-8
    Includes index.
    1. Handicraft. 2. Technology in art. I. Title.
TT157.B356 2010
745.5—dc22
                                    2010014065

Manufactured in China
Illustrations by Will Bryant
Designed by Cody Haltom of Public School

10 9 8 7 6 5 4 3 2 1

Chronicle Books LLC
680 Second Street
San Francisco, California 94107
www.chroniclebooks.com

CE Conforms to ASTM, EN-71, CHPA, and AS/NZS safety standards.

CONTENTS

INTRODUCTION

ONCE UPON A TIME, geeky kids built soapbox derby racers or saved their nickels for comic books (and for sending away for the array of exciting things advertised in the back); a little later, they were reading sci-fi magazines—if they weren't glued to new episodes of *Buck Rogers* or *Star Trek*. And then they were learning BASIC, or playing Pong on their brand-new Ataris (or maybe it was Oregon Trail on a Commodore 64), and then digging quarters out of their piggy banks for the arcade. Play-stations and then Xboxes took their turn on center stage, along with Harry Potter books and graphic novels . . . now, needless to say, there's something for everyone, no matter how old you are: Warcraft, Wiis, and WiFi; comics, cons, and costumes; lively Web sites; and local and global communities bring every facet of geekery to life. The modern age is a thrilling time for geeks—and for crafters—and if you happen to fall into both categories, well, that's even better.

We've come a long way since "geek" meant a carnival sideshow freak and "crafty" meant making enough quilts to keep your entire family warm all winter. These days, geeky and crafty go together like chocolate and peanut butter . . . or pixels and cross-stitch. Being geeky has always been about making and doing things. That's nothing new—kids who went to Space Camp constructed and launched their own model rockets, and D&Ders pains-

takingly hand-drew maps, or painted their own pewter figures. Remember playing video games, taking a Polaroid photo of your high score, sending it in, and proudly sewing the patch you got back on your windbreaker?

These days, all you have to do is visit Maker Faire or check out the lovingly handmade costumes at any con to witness the happy marriage of geek and craft. In this luxurious age, if you want a couple skeins of hand-spun yarn in Gryffindor scarlet and gold, an exact Yoda-green shade of wool felt, or just the right strand of LEDs for the messenger bag project you have in mind, you can track them down pretty darn easily. And if you want to see how someone else made their ASCII cross-stitch or Frogger T-shirt, a spin through Flickr, Craftster, or Etsy lands you a wealth of cool inspiration.

Because of course it's not just the *stuff*, the books and video games and movies . . . it's the fun things we do with it, too—like a LilyPad Arduino Cake (page 123), a Pac-Man Fever Wii-mote Belt and Holster (page 51), or a Vintage Sci-Fi Book Cozy (page 129).

I'm so fortunate to have had some of my favorite crafters contribute their brilliant ideas to this book. Of course, a book of 25 crafty projects that focuses on a mere two dozen geeky genres is just the tip of the iceberg. Hopefully I haven't left out your absolute favorite—it was so hard to narrow it down! But whether you make these projects exactly as they are on the page, or put your own spin on them, I hope you'll find the collection inspiring and adaptable.

Instead of re-creating Tatooine, Hoth, and Endor (page 33), maybe you'll make a set of *Lord of the Rings* terrariums; or after you knit a Jayne-hat-inspired coffee sleeve (page 71), you'll dream up a Tetris pattern for your next one. You can translate a favorite phrase from *Doctor Who* into Morse code and stitch up a quilt secretly spelling it out (see page 117); glue up a set of DNA commemorative plates (see page 19); or decorate a Risk cake (see page 123) for your next game night. . . The possibilities are endless. No matter what your favorite corner of the vast geek kingdom is, you can celebrate it with a craft—for yourself, your friends, or your swaps.

Along with a super-fun mix of craft projects to try, from crochet to woodwork, LED, and embroidery, you'll also hear from some of my favorite geeks, writing about their areas of expertise, such as the DIY of D&D or what it's like to work at Lucasfilm. I also asked everyone who contributed to the book to share their best geeky memory (don't we all have one?), and got some priceless stories.

To get things started, here's mine: *When I was six years old, I begged my dad to take me to see* The Empire Strikes Back, *and one glorious hot, sunny afternoon we headed to the Mission Valley Cinemas to stand in the long snaking line together. We finally settled into our seats, with our popcorn, and the lights went down: the opening moments were the most exciting thing I'd ever seen in my life. (I loved the rest of the movie, but I have to admit that I was so terrified during Luke's lightsaber duel with Darth Vader that I turned around and anxiously watched the projector until I knew Luke was safe back on the* Millenium Falcon.*) Twenty-five years later, buying tickets for a midnight showing of* Revenge of the Sith *and seeing the magnificent opening moments—holding hands with my husband—brought me right back to the first time.*

I'd love to see what you make from the World of Geekcraft collection, so please check out the book's Web site and photo gallery at worldofgeekcraft.com to share your own projects (and geeky memories!). The contributors and I are sharing more crafty ideas, project extras, and resources galore.

Happy Crafting!

Susan

NOT A JeDi Yet: *Easy Projects*

POW! ZAP! MAGNETS

BY Susan Beal

Turn your refrigerator (or the back of your car or anything else magnetic) into a giant comics panel with these simple, eye-catching POW! and ZAP! magnets! Switch up the colors (old-school B&W or grayscale, maybe? I used glitter felt for the red to give added pop to my letters) or phrases (BAM! BIFF!) to suit your inner cartoonist.

⌐◨-◨ GEEK SPEAK

ESSENTIAL COMIC BOOK KNOWLEDGE
by Vincent Morrison

For years, the phenomena of comic books registered with most of the world as 4-color fluffy superhero adventures, with two-dimensional characters for prepubescent boys to idolize. Although that was once upon a time true, comics have grown up, as have their readers. And the rise of independent comic publishers has spawned a comic (r)evolution.

Still, when comics are mentioned, even most constituents of Geekdom will think of two main corporate producers of superhero comics: DC and Marvel.

The universe created by DC (known, aptly enough, as the DC Universe) is the home of such characters as Superman, Wonder Woman, and Batman. In another part of the firmament, the Marvel Universe holds such intellectual properties as the Fantastic Four, Spider-Man, and the X-Men. (Beware, as comic geeks hate it if you accidentally place a character in the wrong universe.) While countless blog wars, IRC conversations, and Twitter skirmishes have been fought comparing and contrasting the two biggest universes (or, to be technical, multiverses), it's arguably safe to just think of DC as a universe of bright colors filled with icons of good and evil, and Marvel as a universe built on darker angst where somewhat good heroes battle somewhat evil villains. Interestingly, there are those who argue that DC is becoming more like Marvel every day, and that both universes are being influenced heavily by the indie-comic universes that surround them. Regardless, familiarize yourself with the worlds, choose your affiliation, and be prepared to defend it.

VINCENT MORRISON *is comic book–obsessed. He's a big fan of the DC Universe, and would prefer that Marvel Zombies never happened. You can find his thoughts on comics, science fiction, and the mysteries of the universe, as well as samples of his music, at Vincentmorrison.com.*

BEST GEEKY MEMORY: *I once met George Takei of Star Trek and managed not to drool on him whilst getting my book signed.*

YOU'LL NEED

Tools

- Photocopier (or pen or pencil and tracing paper)
- Scissors
- Straight pins
- Fabric glue

Materials

- POW! ZAP! Magnets templates
  (in Patterns and Templates)
- One 8½-by-11-in/21.5-by-28-cm sheet each blue,
  yellow, and red felt for construction
- Magnetic sheets with adhesive backing

Note: You can adjust the size of this magnet project to be as teeny-tiny cute or as big and bold as you want. The 4-in/10-cm size provided in the templates is easy to spot from the other side of the room and sturdy enough to hold papers and photos, but you can make these at any scale you like.

INSTRUCTIONS

1 Trace or photocopy and cut out all of the templates. Pin the largest burst to your background color felt (mine was blue) and the medium burst to your base color felt (mine was yellow). Pin the letters and exclamation points to your accent color (mine was glittery red). Cut each shape and letter out of the felt.

2 Glue the base layer burst onto the background layer burst, and then the letters and exclamation point onto the base. Let dry completely.

3 Now peel away the protective paper backing from a magnetic sheet to expose the adhesive. Press the glued felt layers firmly onto the adhesive side. Use the scissors to cut away excess magnet, trimming it very close to the felt edges. (You can also switch the order of the steps, pressing the background color felt into the magnetic sheet and cutting the two layers together.)

4 Repeat to make 3 more magnets. Put your new magnets to work anywhere that needs a comics-style makeover!

Makes 4 magnets

A GIFT FROM THE EMBALMER TOTE BAG

BY Shelbi Roach

The Warcrafts community at WoW.com voted on their all-time favorite craft projects to include in this book, and Shelbi's fantastic tote bag was the winner! Simple felt appliqués bring this bag spookily to life. Check out the marvelous archive of World of Warcraft–inspired projects at the site, including graphic bleach stencil shirts, Murky and Murloc plushies, and even DIY potions and ooze, for plenty more crafts to keep you busy.

You can easily adapt the embellishments for other size bags, if you like.

YOU'LL NEED

Tools

- Photocopier
- Scissors
- Straight pins
- Wax paper
- Craft glue

Materials

- A Gift from the Embalmer Tote Bag templates (in Patterns and Templates)
- One 8½-by-11-in/21.5-by-28-cm sheet each black, red, pink, ivory, white, and charcoal gray felt
- 1 plain 9-by-11-in/23-by-28-cm tote bag

INSTRUCTIONS

1   Photocopy, enlarging 35 percent and cut out all of the templates, leaving the white area on the right eye uncut for now.

2   Pin the templates onto the corresponding colors of felt as shown and cut out the pieces. To cut out the center of the right eye, it's easiest to fold the eye over and cut a tiny slit in the center, then cut out an almond shape.

3   From the gray felt, cut one 11-in/28-cm-long strip and a number of small bars, each about ½ in/12 mm wide. You should have enough small bars to spread out evenly along the longer piece.

4   Place a piece of wax paper inside the tote bag. This will keep any glue that leaks through from getting on the other side of the bag.

5   Lay the pieces of felt on the bag to get a good idea of placement, following the photo of the finished bag for guidance.

6   Once you're satisfied, glue the layered pieces of felt to one another and then glue them to the bag.

7   Trim off any excess and let dry completely.

Makes 1 embellished tote

SHELBI ROACH *has always been a geek at heart. She's currently working on WoW add-on interface designs and filling out her design line called Minitarz—original creations of Blizzard, Marvel, and Nintendo characters. She and her husband run a World of Warcraft blog called the Bronze Kettle, devoted to IRL WoW recipes, fan art, and their in-game experiences.*

BEST GEEKY MEMORY: *Marrying the guy I met online. Now we have two kids we enjoy playing games with, whether it's World of Warcraft with the oldest or Plants vs. Zombies with the youngest.*

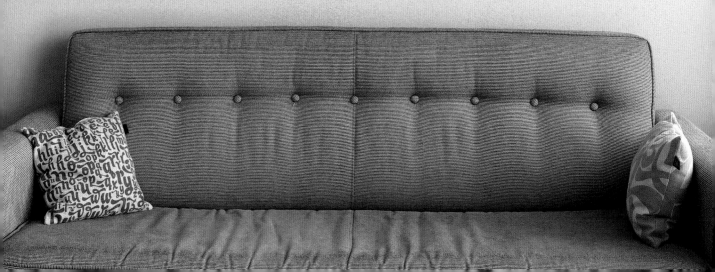

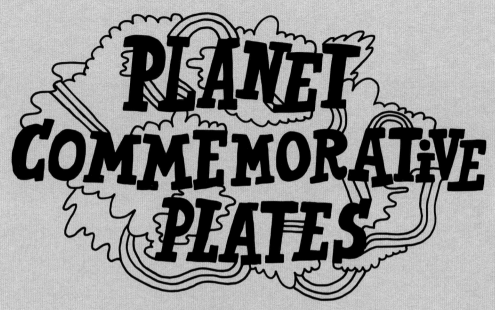

PLANET COMMEMORATIVE PLATES

BY GARTH JOHNSON

Modern technology means that we no longer have to rely on the Franklin Mint to release collector plates of our favorite bands or television shows. Anyone with a photocopier or inkjet printer and access to a thrift store can take matters into their own hands and create one-of-a-kind collector's plates—a perfect addition to any office or child's room. This recipe yields a fantastic set of space-inspired planet plates, but you can celebrate any geeky favorites in this majestic medium.

Any white ceramic plates you find in thrift stores or garage sales will work for this project. You might want to gather an assortment of sizes and styles to make things interesting. And remember, these embellished plates are for decorative use only—once you fancy them up, they're no longer food-safe.

YOU'LL NEED

- Rubbing alcohol
- Computer with photo-editing software
- Clear acrylic spray paint such as Krylon (not shellac-based)
- Scissors
- Soaking pan (large enough to accommodate all your decals)
- Warm water
- Sponge or paper towel
- X-acto knife (optional)
- Permanent marker

- A set of old plates
- Images to use in your designs
- Decal paper and materials (see Notes, opposite)
- Plate hangers (optional)

INSTRUCTIONS

1 Clean your chosen plates well with rubbing alcohol so that the decals will set nicely.

2 Collect the planet images you want to use and get them into your computer—scan images from books and/or magazines, or get online. One great source for royalty-free images of planets is NASA, at nasa.gov/multimedia/imagegallery. Look for high-resolution images that can be enlarged without becoming fuzzy or jagged. Use Photoshop or other photo-editing software to size your images to the right diameter to fit on your plates.

3 Next, make the decals to decorate your plate. (If

you've ever put together a model car, these decals function in exactly the same way.) If using Lazertran, follow the manufacturer's directions to print on an inkjet printer. If using Bel-Decal, use a color laser printer or high-end color photocopier to print your images on the decal sheets.

4   Now that you've got your images printed on the decal paper, it's time to apply a cover coat that will allow you to transfer the images to your plates. In a well-ventilated area, spray a very light coat of the clear acrylic spray paint onto your decals. Be careful—a heavy coat will smear the ink. After the decals have dried for 5 to 10 minutes, spray them with another, slightly thicker coat of paint and let dry for 30 to 45 minutes. Repeat with 1 or 2 more coats until you have an even, glossy coat. Let the decals dry for at least 2 or up to 12 hours before applying them to the plates.

5   Cut out the decals. Fill the soaking pan with warm water and place the decals in the warm pan to soak, arranging them in a single layer. If your decals crack, then you need to apply another coat of acrylic and start over. The decals should release fully from the paper in about 30 seconds. Working with 1 decal and 1 plate at a time, take the paper and decal out of the water together and carefully slide the decal onto a plate, acrylic side up.

6   Use the sponge or paper towel to work any air bubbles out of the decal, starting from the middle of the plate and working the bubbles outward. Depending on how concave your plate is, you'll inevitably have some waves and creases on the edge of your decal. You can minimize these by carefully cutting them with an X-acto knife. They will also shrink as they dry.

7   After the plates have dried completely, you may want to apply a final coat of acrylic to the fronts. Once they are dry, don't forget to sign and number the backs with a permanent marker.

8   Find a place to display your work! To hang the plates, attach plate hangers on the back; you can find these at nearly any dollar or hardware store. Alternatively, prop them on easels or picture shelves, or use them to decorate a desk, coffee table, dresser, etc.

Makes as many commemorative planets as you have plates!

Notes: There are two easy options for creating the decals; both are a kind of paper called "water slide." The first is a product called Lazertran, specially made to create decals using an inkjet printer. You can purchase the decal paper directly from the company at lazertran.com.

The second product is called Bel-Decal, basically just paper coated with a gum that dissolves in water, allowing you to transfer your image. This is the paper that nearly all decals are printed on; you can purchase it inexpensively from Bel-Decal at beldecal.com. You'll have to use a color laser printer or high-end color photocopier to print your images on the decal sheets. I always put my images on a thumb drive or disc and take them, along with the decal paper, to my local copy shop. You might have to convince them that the paper won't jam their machine (it won't).

GARTH JOHNSON *is an artist, educator, and writer who lives in Eureka, California, and teaches at the College of the Redwoods. Garth brings his own brand of geeky ferocity to his Web site, Extremecraft.com, and his first book,* 1000 Ideas for Creative Reuse. *Look for his Extreme Craft Roadshow at a venue near you.*

BEST GEEKY MEMORY: *The only video game I ever "beat" was the aptly named Commodore 64 game Bop 'n' Wrestle.*

CYLON HOODIE

BY Heather Mann

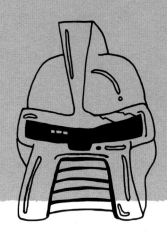

Channel your inner Cylon Centurion by adding a menacing visor and uniform patches to your favorite hoodie. If you're afraid of your sewing machine, this embellishment project can also be completed with a needle and thread. Advanced crafters might want to add an LED component for the ominously sweeping red-eye effect.

YOU'LL NEED

Tools

- Photocopier
- Scissors
- Scotch tape
- Spray adhesive such as 3M Super 77
- Sewing machine or hand-sewing needle
- Straight pins
- Pinking shears (optional)

Materials

- Cylon Hoodie templates (in Patterns and Templates)
- One 8½-by-11-in/21.5-by-28-cm sheet red felt or red vinyl (I used a vinyl place mat)
- One 8½-by-11-in/21.5-by-28-cm sheet black or gray felt, to match the hoodie
- Thread
- Black or gray hooded sweatshirt
- ¼ yd/23 cm gray polar fleece
- ½ yd/46 cm quilted metallic no-fray costume fabric, or equivalent

INSTRUCTIONS

1. Photocopy, enlarging per instructions on template pages, and cut out all of the Cylon Hoodie templates. Tape the Cylon Eye template to the red felt or vinyl, then cut out the eye piece. Use the Cylon Visor template to cut 2 visor pieces out of the gray or black felt.

2. In a well-ventilated area, spray adhesive over the back of the red eye piece and affix it to one of the visor pieces as shown in the photo. Topstitch the eye piece to the felt with a sewing machine or by hand.

3. Pin the two visor pieces right sides together and stitch around the curve, using a ½-in/12-mm seam allowance. Turn the visor inside out, so that the right sides are now facing out, and topstitch across the remaining open side, and then again around the curve.

4. Pin the visor to the center of the hood, then stitch it on.

5. Using the remaining templates, cut 2 *each* from the gray fleece: Cylon Shoulder Cap, Chest Accent, and AB Patch. Cut 1 *each* from the metallic fabric: Helmet Piece and Back Panel (be sure to place the dotted line of the back panel on a fabric fold so that you cut a panel twice as long as the pattern piece). Finally, cut 2 Upper Chest Patches from the metallic fabric. If your metallic fabric is woven (and therefore frayable), you will want to edge those patches with pinking shears to keep them from unraveling once they're sewn on.

6. Using the photo as a guideline for placement, pin and topstitch the pattern pieces onto the hoodie in this order: fleece shoulder cap pieces; metallic upper chest patches; and then fleece chest accent pieces, layered diagonally over the metallic upper chest patches.

7. Next, pin and topstitch the fleece AB patches below the upper chest patches, and pin and stitch the metallic helmet piece onto the hood and the visor you sewed on in steps 3 and 4. Finally, unfold the back panel so it lies flat. Pin it in place on the back of the hoodie, and topstitch it down.

Makes 1 hoodie

HEATHER MANN *is the founder of Dollarstorecrafts.com, editor and publisher of CROQZine.com, a print zine devoted to hip crafting and indie business, and the founding editor of CraftFail.com, a community blog devoted to sharing our not-so-successful crafting attempts. She is also the mother of three little boys whom she hopes to train in the ways of the geek.*

BEST GEEKY MEMORY: *Several years ago I went to my first grown-up Halloween party, and I dressed as the Japanese monster character Domo. I felt like a huge geek because the people at the party were mostly dressed as scantily clad versions of various Halloween clichés, and had no idea who the grimacing brown monster was supposed to be.*

OREGON TRAIL CROSS-STITCH

BY John Lohman

Relive your epic elementary-school wagon journeys across the frontier with this nostalgic needlework project depicting a game-hunting scene from the classic Oregon Trail educational video game. The black background fabric brings the state-of-the-art 1980s computer screen effect vividly to life—space bar not included!

YOU'LL NEED

Tools

- Embroidery needle
- Scissors

Materials

- Oregon Trail cross-stitch pattern (below)
- Aida 14-count (or the size of your choice; see pages 146 and 147) cross-stitch fabric, in black
- DMC embroidery floss: 310 black, 702 kelly green, 740 tangerine, 5200 snow white
- Frame of your choice

INSTRUCTIONS

Follow the counted cross-stitch pattern, stitching the darker parts of the design first, until you've completed the entire design. Frame as desired.

Makes 1 framed cross-stitch

JOHN LOHMAN *is an avid cross-stitcher, classic gamer, and the founder of Spritestitch.com, a video game craft blog. He lives in Grants Pass, Oregon.*

BEST GEEKY MEMORY: *The many afternoons playing Beyond Zork with my family on our Apple.*

👓 GEEK SPEAK

MAY THE FORCE BE WITH YOUR GLUE GUN
by Bonnie Burton

Steampunk R2-D2, Jedi fashions, and AT-AT baby strollers are nothing new to me. Over the years working for Lucasfilm, I've been lucky enough to witness our fans' creativity firsthand. Whether it's the elaborate costumes sewn by the Rebel Legion, professional-standard stormtrooper armor modeled by the 501st Legion, working droids by the R2 Builders, and adorable toys made by moms, dads, grandparents, teens, and crafty kids—I'm always impressed by the talents of *Star Wars* fans around the world.

The *Star Wars* films became a reality in a large part thanks to the crafty crew of ILM model makers and creature supervisors who made a myriad of cool vehicles, intricately detailed sets, and fantastical creatures. Because of the DIY spirit of director George Lucas and his crew, many fans were inspired to make their own tributes to *Star Wars*, from TIE fighters constructed out of paper cups to Death Star birthday cakes!

There's something extra-special about us geeky crafters. Not only do we gladly cover ourselves in glitter for the sake of a sparkly project, we also can't help but share our ideas with others. At any given comic book or sci-fi convention, I constantly run into fellow crafters who are more than eager to share their R2-D2 pillow patterns or Han Solo embroidery samplers. Go on any crafting site or forum and do a search for *Star Wars*, and you'll soon find fans swapping ideas on how to make stormtrooper action figure jewelry and crocheted lightsaber cozies.

I can't help but wonder if geeky crafters are guided to each other by the Force. There's a certain bond we feel when showing off our Boba Fett bean art portraits or Mos Eisley Cantina dioramas. Never underestimate the power of the craft side!

BONNIE BURTON *is a San Francisco author and crafter, and senior editor at Lucasfilm. Her books include* The Star Wars Craft Book, Draw Star Wars: The Clone Wars, *and* You Can Draw: Star Wars, *among others. Check out her craft projects on Starwars.com, and on her site Grrl.com.*

BEST GEEKY MEMORY: *I was inducted as an Honorary Member into the stormtrooper costuming group the 501st Legion by a trio called the League of Extraordinary Troopers, which included stormtroopers dressed as Sherlock Holmes, Pancho Villa, and Kato from* The Green Hornet.

STAR WARS TERRARIUMS

BY Susan Beal

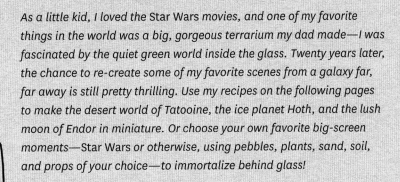

As a little kid, I loved the Star Wars movies, and one of my favorite things in the world was a big, gorgeous terrarium my dad made—I was fascinated by the quiet green world inside the glass. Twenty years later, the chance to re-create some of my favorite scenes from a galaxy far, far away is still pretty thrilling. Use my recipes on the following pages to make the desert world of Tatooine, the ice planet Hoth, and the lush moon of Endor in miniature. Or choose your own favorite big-screen moments—Star Wars or otherwise, using pebbles, plants, sand, soil, and props of your choice—to immortalize behind glass!

Some layers or plantings call for powdered charcoal because it helps drain and filter within your terrarium. You can find powdered charcoal at art supply stores and online.

YOU'LL NEED

Tools

- Chopsticks or bamboo skewers for adjusting your arrangements
- Teaspoon
- Scissors
- Pencil
- Craft glue

Materials

FOR CONSTRUCTION
- Photocopier (or pen or pencil and tracing paper)
- 3 large screw-top or other jars with a tight-fitting lid (mine were 9 in/23 cm tall and 16 in/40.5 cm in circumference)
- Luke Skywalker, Han Solo, Princess Leia, and Wicket the Ewok action figures (I couldn't stand to leave C-3PO, R2-D2, and Yoda out of things, so they are part of the display—add any others of your choice, as you like)
- Small lengths of thin bamboo skewer, 2 per action figure, about 1 in/2.5 cm long, cut from the tips

FOR TATOOINE
- Medium-sized honey-colored pebbles
- Powdered charcoal
- 1 or 2 lithop plants or other succulents
- Honey-colored sand
- Tatooine Suns templates (in Patterns and Templates)
- Small pieces of orange or red and pale tan cardstock

FOR HOTH
- Snowspeeder templates (in Patterns and Templates)
- Medium-sized white pebbles
- White sand
- Small white jagged rocks, white quartz, and coral

FOR ENDOR
- Chocolate-brown pebbles
- Powdered charcoal
- 1 leafy succulent plant
- Potting soil
- Moss
- 1 small piece tree branch, about 4½ in/11 cm long and 1 in/2.5 cm in diameter

INSTRUCTIONS

1 Wash and dry the jars thoroughly. Have your action figures and a good supply of chopsticks or bamboo skewers ready to use as needed for support or positioning the parts of the scene. Insert a 1-in/2.5-cm piece of bamboo, pointed side down, into the holes in each figure's feet; these will act as the anchors when you add the figures to the terrariums.

2 *To make the Tatooine terrarium*, add about 1 in/2.5 cm of the honey-colored pebbles to the bottom of a jar. Using the teaspoon, make 1 or 2 small recesses (as many as the lithop plants you are using) in the stones, then add a small spoonful of charcoal to each one. Insert the lithop plant or plants (or other succulents), nestling the root ball(s) in the charcoal.

3 Add the honey-colored sand to a depth of about 2 in/5 cm, nudging it so it surrounds the plants, and then heap it higher, to about 2.5 in/6 cm, on one side of the jar. Place Luke Skywalker on the high ground of the mounded sand.

4 Trace or photocopy and cut out the 2 Suns templates. Trace 1 sun on each color of cardstock, then cut out the suns. Glue the 2 suns onto the outside of the glass, offset (as shown on page 34) and above the "horizon," so that Luke is looking out at them from his vantage point.

5 *To make the Hoth terrarium*, trace or photocopy and cut out the 2 Snowspeeder templates. Glue them back-to-back and set aside to dry completely.

6 Add about 1 in/2.5 cm of the white pebbles to the bottom of the second jar. Add white sand on top of the pebbles to a depth of about 2 in/5 cm. Place a chunk of white quartz on one side, nestled into the sand. Add small jagged white pebbles as a top layer all around the white quartz, and add a coral or other white element to the back of the jar, if you like.

7 Place Han, with arm waving, centered on the side opposite from the chunk of white quartz.

8 Glue the two-sided snowspeeder onto the outside of the glass at an angle in front of Han.

9 *To make the Endor terrarium*, add about 1 in/2.5 cm of the chocolate-brown pebbles to the bottom of the last jar, then a thin layer of charcoal about ¼ in/6 mm deep.

10 Tuck the leafy succulent at the back of the scene, add a pinch or two of potting soil, and pack firmly to cover and support. Scatter more potting soil as needed and plant moss to surround the plant and to an overall height of about 2 in/5 cm. Place the tree-branch "log" diagonally in front of the succulent. Heap a small section of moss and soil against the wall of the jar at one end of the log to create a slightly higher ground.

11 Place Princess Leia so she is sitting, or leaning, on the opposite side of the log, and place Wicket on the mound, brandishing his spear.

Makes 3 terrariums

Note for terrarium purists: I didn't actually add plants to my Hoth (given its famously inhospitable climate), but decorated the scene with coral and quartz for an icy effect. If you want to try adding a plant to the scene, I suggest a white or pale-colored air plant.

Note for *Star Wars* purists: Leia's original combat poncho will quickly mildew in Endor's lush ecosystem, so take that off before placing your figure in the scene.

GEEK SPEAK

IN THE FUTURE THERE IS JUST ONE GIRL AND OTHER THINGS I LEARNED FROM SCIENCE FICTION

by Chelsea Cain

I can remember the first time I played with *Star Wars* action figures. It was 1977 — I was five years old — and I watched a kid named Ethan Bolt melt stormtroopers over his parents' backyard trash-burning barrel. Stormtroopers were a dime a dozen back then. Their white plastic armor blackened and bubbled. Maybe it was the toxic fumes, but I was hooked. He gave me his Princess Leia. She was useless to him. A girl.

Did you ever notice how there was always only one girl in the future? *Star Trek* had Uhura. *Buck Rogers* had Col. Wilma Deering. *Flash Gordon* had Dale Arden. *Doctor Who* had Sarah Jane Smith.

You'd think I might have found this alarming. Had a virus wiped out 90 percent of human women? But I loved it. All those neighborhood Hans and Bucks, they needed me.

I learned to wield a lightsaber, relay communication from Star Fleet, and run in high-heel boots.

It sure beat playing "house," a game I hated because I was tall and the other girls always made me be "the dad."

Those girls had no interest in the prime directive.

They just wanted to watch *Little House on the Prairie*.

Then a horrible thing happened: Middle School. All the boys packed up their action figures and started watching *Charles in Charge*. If they found some other geek fest (D&D?), they didn't invite me.

I still watched the shows. I told no one. I knew it was wrong. Sci-fi was something to be done in private with the curtains drawn.

I didn't come out until college. (I had accidentally named every single actor who'd played Doctor Who, in chronological order. It just slipped out.)

These days there are sci-fi shows with five or six females. Someone must have invented a vaccine for that terrible virus. My four-year-old daughter will have plenty of kick-ass space women role models.

She's already got one. A few weeks ago, I presented her with her very first Princess Leia action figure.

CHELSEA CAIN *is the author of* New York Times *best-selling thrillers* Evil at Heart, Sweetheart, *and* Heartsick. *Her books have been published in over twenty languages, and named among Stephen King's top ten books of 2008. She is also co-author of the geek-i-riffic* Does This Cape Make Me Look Fat? Pop Psychology for Superheros, *as well as other titles. She still believes that Tom Baker was the best Doctor Who.*

BEST GEEKY MEMORY: *I have been to the James T. Kirk memorial in Riverside, Iowa. (His "future birthplace.") And it was kinda moving.*

DI: 4815162342

PEAS

LOST Tin-Can Telephones and Swan Station Logbook

By Ryan and Lucy Berkley

These improvised communication tools are such easy craft projects, it's hard to understand why the citizens of the Island didn't make them for themselves. Tin-can telephones give you the analog ability to communicate with your fellow castaways from across a jungle, while speaking quietly enough to avoid detection by the Others. Try it and you'll see. Meanwhile, you can record your observations in your Swan Station logbook.

If you do not have any immediate communication needs, you can also use the cans for holding your pens and pencils or a bouquet of flowers, or even tie them to the back of the car at your geeky friend's wedding.

Detail of stitch binding.

YOU'LL NEED

for the LOST tin-can telephones

Tools

- Photocopier
- Scissors
- Elmer's glue or a glue stick
- Hammer and nail

Materials

- 2 tin cans, emptied and washed thoroughly, with one end removed and one end intact (ours measured 4½ in/ 11.5 cm tall and 3 in/7.5 cm in diameter; if yours are bigger or smaller, you may need to adjust the label dimensions accordingly)
- *LOST* Yams and Peas Label templates (both in Patterns and Templates)
- 10 to 20 ft/3 to 6 m of string, twine, or any type of sturdy line you might find in the jungle (we used a natural fiber green twine from the hardware store)

INSTRUCTIONS

1. Remove the labels from your tin cans and set aside. Copy the *LOST* Yams and Peas Label (in Patterns and Templates). Cut out each image and re-copy each onto its own sheet of white paper. Using the labels from your own cans as a guideline for size, center each one over the Yams and Peas images and trace them, adding an extra 1 in/2.5 cm to the width.

2. Cut out the labels and wrap one around each can, gluing it down where the paper overlaps.

3. Using a hammer and nail, puncture the center of the end of each can. Make sure the hole is large enough to fit the string.

4. With the open ends of the cans facing away from one another, feed the string through the hole in each can, tying a double knot at each end so that the knots are inside the cans.

5. Give your friend one of the cans and walk away from each other until the line is tight. It's very important for the line to be tight and for nothing to be touching it! Now you can talk into one can and your friend can listen in the other, and vice versa. It works! Try flicking the string to make other signals to each other, too.

Makes 1 pair of two-way telephones

YOU'LL NEED
for the swan station logbook

Tools
- System Failure printout and Swan Station Logbook Cover template (both in Patterns and Templates)
- Photocopier (or pen or pencil and tracing paper)
- Ruler
- Pencil
- Bone folder (or the back end of a pen, if you can't find a bone folder in your hatch)
- Sturdy needle

Materials
- Five 8½-by-11-in/21.5-by-28-cm sheets regular weight printer paper
- One 8½-by-11-in/21.5-by-28-cm medium- or heavy-weight cardstock (make sure it's not too thick to run through your printer or photocopier)
- Thread to match cardstock color

INSTRUCTIONS

1 Copy the System Failure printout onto the 5 sheets of regular-weight paper, and copy the Swan Station Logbook Cover template onto the sheet of cardstock. The printer paper will be your interior pages, and the cardstock will be your cover.

2 Fold the cover in half crosswise, and set it aside. Now fold the interior pages in half crosswise, one at a time, with the text side of each page facing outward, to make 10 half-width pages. The cover and interior pages should now be 4¼ by 5½ in/11 by 14 cm folded, and 8½ by 5½ in/21.5 by 14 cm unfolded.

3 Tuck the interior pages inside the cover, with the text reading from bottom to top. With the pages inside, mark the notebook's spine and use the bone folder to make a sharp, clean crease down the center.

4 Use the needle to pierce three holes along the crease, through all layers: one in the middle and two 1½ in/4 cm from each of the edges.

5 Thread the needle and knot the thread securely. Starting inside the book, feed the needle and thread through all layers via the center hole, leaving about 3 in/7.5 cm loose inside. Outside the spine, thread the needle back through the top hole. Back inside the book, bring the needle up through the bottom hole. Lastly, thread the needle from the outside of the book back through the center hole (careful not to split the initial thread). Tie the two ends together in a square knot, and cut off excess thread.

6 Give the spine of your book another pass with the bone folder and let it rest overnight under a heavier book or other weight to keep the cover flat.

7 Gather lots of clues and diagrams to help solve the mysteries of the Island.

Makes 1 logbook

RYAN AND LUCY BERKLEY *are a husband and wife duo from Portland, Oregon, who enjoy many of the geekier things in life as well as running their art business, Berkley Illustration. Ryan is a bona fide comics nerd while Lucy tends to obsess over puzzles and riddles. Check them out at Berkleyillustration.etsy.com or Letsshare.typepad.com.*

BEST GEEKY MEMORY: *We've twice traveled halfway across the country to attend Star Wars conventions. While there, Ryan waited in line for seven hours to get an exclusive George Lucas action figure and Lucy got a crush on every Chewbacca.*

ONE UP: *Intermediate Projects*

MARiO MAGRiTTE

BY John Lohman

Mario meets Surrealism in this inspired and delightful cross-stitch design. The elegant color shading and clever caption contrast beautifully with the nostalgic graphic blockiness. Frame this one for your game room.

this ain't a pipe...

👓 GEEK SPEAK

THE RESURGENCE OF ATARI AND NINTENDO
by Renee Asher

If you were a kid in the eighties, Atari was cool because it was all there was—starting in 1978, Atari held the market in awesome 8-bit at home entertainment. As the eighties progressed, Nintendo entered the scene with games like Donkey Kong and Mario Bros. Atari faded into the background. In the new millennium, it seems like every time you turn around there is a newer, more sophisticated video game console on the market; games like Halo take individual game play to a level that a kid playing Pac-Man in 1980 could never have imagined.

Today's teenagers have amazing 3-D graphics, intense game plots, and levels that last forever. Yet from belt buckles shaped like the original Nintendo controllers to track jackets with the Atari logo and Pac-Man apps, Atari and the original NES still seem to be everywhere. Hipster kids wearing fedoras and skinny jeans are just as likely to be sporting a Donkey Kong T-shirt. Of course the obvious question is, why the nostalgia?

A big part of the renewed popularity of Atari and NES games lies within the breakthrough idea that it's actually cool to be geeky. The word "geek" has transitioned from describing someone wearing a pocket protector to someone who is hip, in the know, and totally capable of keeping up with technology. With new video game consoles, cell phones, and computers coming out faster than most people can keep up with, being a geek has its advantages. As loads of average Joes jump on the geek-chic bandwagon, it seems the hardcore geeks feel the need to separate themselves; perhaps wearing an old Atari logo is a way of saying, "Yeah, I was here first."

RENEE ASHER *is a contributing editor for Geekcrafts.com, where she spotlights the best in video games projects. She lives in Joshua Tree, California. Her writing can be found at ReneeAsher.com.*

BEST GEEKY MEMORY: *When my husband and I spent a day at the Coventry Travel Museum's Doctor Who Exhibit. I got to "pet" the real K-9!*

YOU'LL NEED

Tools

- Scissors
- Embroidery needle

Materials

- Mario Magritte cross-stitch pattern (below)
- Aida 14-count (or the size of your choice; see page 146 and 147) cross-stitch fabric, in oatmeal
- DMC embroidery floss: 310 black, 779 cocoa-dark, 3864 mocha beige-light
- Frame of your choice

INSTRUCTIONS

Follow the counted cross-stitch pattern, stitching the darker parts of the design first, until you've completed the entire design. Frame as desired.

Makes 1 framed cross-stitch

For more about John, see page 29.

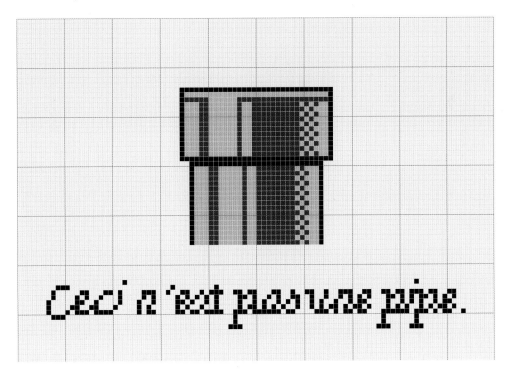

PAC-MAN FEVER Wii-MOTE BELT AND HOLSTER

BY Cathy Pitters

Carry your Wii-mote in style with this fantastic retro-inspired piece embellished with Pac-Man and power pellets. Whether you grew up saving your quarters for the arcade or putting Wii games at the top of your Christmas list, this belt and holster are perfect for video game lovers of every era.

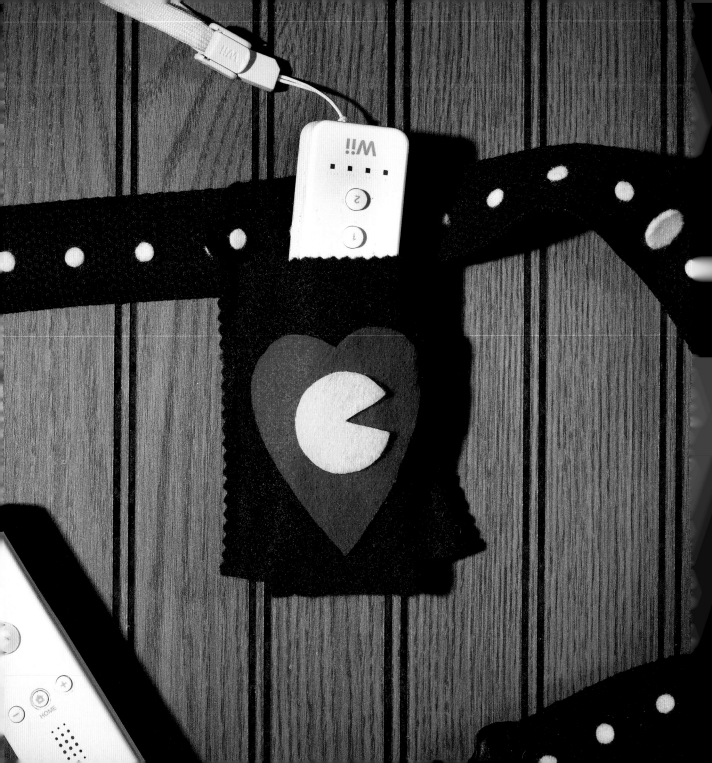

YOU'LL NEED

Tools

- Photocopier (or pen or pencil and tracing paper)
- Tape measure
- Straight pins
- Sewing machine
- Thread
- Scissors
- Pinking shears (optional)
- Small, sharp scissors (optional)
- ¼-in/6-mm hole punch (optional)
- ⅛-in/3-mm hole punch (optional)
- Fabric glue

Materials

- 1½ to 2 yd/1.5 to 2 m cotton webbing, 1½ in/4 cm wide, black or the color of your choice
- 1 slide-release belt buckle that accommodates 1½ in/ 4 cm webbing
- Pac-man Fever Wii-mote Holster pattern (in Patterns and Templates)
- One 15-by-5-in/38-by-12-cm piece black felt
- Wii-mote embellishment templates (in Patterns and Templates)
- Small pieces of red, white, yellow, light blue, light pink, and royal blue felt

INSTRUCTIONS

1 First decide how large you want your belt to be, keeping in mind that it will usually be worn on top of clothing and will be adjustable. (I decided that my belt would fit up to a 40-in/101.5-cm waist. Adding 4 in/ 10 cm to account for folding over and finishing off the ends, I cut my webbing to 44 in/112 cm.)

2 Your buckle should have one side where the belt will be adjustable and one side that will be stationary. Slide the webbing through the stationary side, position-ing the buckle about 2 in/5 cm from the end. Fold the webbing over, tuck the unfinished end under, and pin it in place. Now use a sewing machine to stitch a small rectangle shape to secure the layers of webbing in place.

3 Take up the other end of the webbing and fold it over about 2 in/5 cm from the end, then tuck the unfinished edge under. Machine-stitch a small rectangle shape to secure the layers of webbing on that end. Feed this end through the adjustable side of the buckle—now you have a belt!

4 Trace or photocopy and cut out the Holster pattern. Pin it to the black felt and cut it out. Since felt can have some give to it, it's a good idea to sew around the perimeter of the pattern piece ¼ in/6 mm from the edge to reinforce it before assembling.

5 To make the loop that will hold the holster on the belt, fold the top flap of the pattern piece over toward the back 2 in/5 cm (see the fold lines on the Holster pattern). Tuck the end under about ½ in/12 mm at the upper fold line, and pin it in place. Make sure the loop is at least 1½ in/4 cm tall, so the belt will fit through. Machine-stitch a small rectangle shape to secure the loop in place (shown as a shaded area on the pattern).

6 If you'd like a decorative edge, cut along the bottom edge of the holster piece with pinking shears before folding it into shape, then fold the holster piece roughly in half, along the lowest fold line on the pattern. The bottom corners should meet up. Machine-stitch both sides of the holster piece, leaving a ¼-in/6-mm seam allowance. Trim these 2 sides with pinking shears for further flair (optional but super cute!).

7 Now assemble the belt and holster. Slide the adjustable end of the belt (without the buckle) through the loop on the back of the finished holster. It should be a snug fit so that the holster will stay in place. Next, slide the end of the belt through the adjustable side of the buckle, and you have a finished—but undecorated!—belt and holster.

8 To embellish your holster, trace or photocopy and cut out the ghost, heart, and Pac-Man templates. (Smaller scissors work best, as some of the pieces are tiny!) Pin these patterns to felt and cut them out. Use the ¼-in/6-mm hole punch to cut out the white Pac-dots and ghost eyes and the ⅛-in/3-mm hole punch for the tiny blue ghost pupils. (This is a HUGE time-saver.) You can also use the paper templates for these, if you prefer.

9 Depending on the size of your belt and your personal taste, you can use any combination of Pac-Men, ghosts, Pac-dots, and Power Pellets (the slightly larger white dots). For reference, these are the embellishments used in the finished project in the photo on page 52:
- Belt—1 small yellow Pac Man, 1 light pink ghost (Pinky), 1 red ghost (Blinky), 1 light blue ghost (Inky), 2 large white dots (Power Pellets), 41 small white Pac-dots (including 6 from the ghost eyes), and 6 tiny royal blue dots (for ghost pupils)
- Holster—1 large yellow Pac Man and 1 red heart

10 Lay the blank belt and holster on a flat surface, and place the felt pieces on top to get a good idea of placement. Play around with the layout, keeping in mind where the holster will fall on your waist—for example, are you a lefty or a righty? (I put a ghost on my belt buckle and positioned my white dots about 1 in/2.5 cm apart along the belt and also along the holster loop. I embellished the holster with a large red heart and yellow Pac Man, but you can get creative with your own personalized version. Do you prefer Ms. Pac-Man? Add a red bow and red lips!)

11 When your design layout is final, use fabric glue to adhere all of the felt pieces in place. Let dry completely. You now have your very own retro-inspired Pac-Man Fever Wii-mote Belt and Holster!

Makes 1 Wii-mote belt and holster

CATHY PITTERS *is a mom, artist, and seamstress who lives in Portland, Oregon, with her family. She runs her own handmade business, Bossanovababy.com, and is one-fourth of the women's collective PDX Super Crafty, who wrote* Super Crafty *together in 2005. She also co-organizes Crafty Wonderland (Craftywonderland .com), a twice yearly art and craft event.*

BEST GEEKY MEMORY: *I have a distinct memory of the first time I saw the original* Star Wars *movie in a theater. It was 1977 and I was nine years old. I remember the opening sequence . . . "A long time ago in a galaxy far, far away . . . " then the words telling the story as they moved away from me and up the screen. I had never seen anything like it! The movie blew my nine-year-old mind! It's been fun to watch my son see the movies for the first time and enjoy them just as much.*

d20 DELUXE

BY Susan Beal

Make yourself a sparkly dice necklace and earrings set to attract plenty of treasure and luck! Drill through 20-sided dice and connect them with 20-gauge wire for perfect necklace alchemy. Make sure to leave your 20s proudly front and center, of course. I added 7 in/18 cm of gold chain to the length created by the sum of the dice's widths, but you can make the finished necklace longer or shorter as you like, by adjusting the amount of chain you use or changing up the number of dice.

The d8 earrings are more of an instant-gratification craft—no power tools required.

YOU'LL NEED
for the Necklace

Tools

- Wire cutters
- Tape measure
- Round-nose pliers
- Flat-nose pliers

Materials

- 1 spool 20-gauge gold wire
- Nine 20-sided dice, drilled through
  (see Note, page 60)
- 7 in/18 cm gold chain of your choice
- 1 small gold jump ring
- Gold clasp (hook or lobster style)
- 2 large round or oval gold jump rings
- One 4-sided die, drilled through

INSTRUCTIONS

1 Cut 9 pieces of 20-gauge wire, each about 2.5 in/ 6 cm long. Using the round-nose pliers, form a medium-sized loop at one end of one of the wire pieces. Now slide the wire through a drilled die and form a second loop at the other end the same way to hold it securely in place. Trim any excess wire. This is your first connector.

2 Repeat step 1 with another piece of wire and another die, but link the second loop to a loop on your first finished piece before closing it. (Or you could make all your dice into connectors first, and then open the loops with flat-nose pliers to link them.)

3 Make 7 more d20s into connectors, linking them with the first two, until you have nine dice "beads" joined in a chain-like row.

4 Cut the chain into two 2½-in/6-cm pieces and two 1-in/2.5-cm pieces. Gently open an outer wire loop on your 9-die centerpiece, and slip it through the first link of a 2½-in/6-cm chain, closing it securely afterward. Repeat with the second 2½-in/6-cm piece of chain on the other side of the centerpiece.

5 Use your pliers to open the small jump ring and add the clasp to one end of the necklace chain, closing it securely afterwards.

6 Open your 2 large jump rings. Add one to the last link of the chain on the opposite side of the necklace from the clasp. Link a 1-in/2.5-cm piece of chain through it and close the ring securely. Add the second large jump ring to the new end of the chain, and add the last 1-in/2.5-cm piece of chain to that before closing. You now have a longer chain on this side with 2 rings to fasten the clasp to, which makes the necklace adjustable.

7 Cut 1 more 2½-in/6-cm piece of wire and repeat step 1 to turn your 4-sided die into a connector. Open the top (triangle-point) loop and join it to the open end of the chain as a dangling ornament—not for clasping, just for decoration.

Makes 1 adjustable necklace

Note: My friend Ryan used a ³⁄₃₂-inch drill bit on the points of our dice, which created a perfect-sized hole for 20-gauge wire to pass through neatly.

YOU'LL NEED
for the earrings

Tools

· A bowl of uncooked rice
· Hypo-cement glue
· Wire cutters

Materials

· Two 8-sided dice
· 2 gold bead caps
· Gold chain of your choice (I used 2 in/5 cm total)
· Gold earring wires (I used leverbacks)
· 2 small gold jump rings

INSTRUCTIONS

1 Place the two d8s in the bowl of rice (or another spot where they'll stay in place for gluing), top points up. Add a generous dab of glue to the top of each one and press a bead cap onto each. Let them dry completely.

2 Cut a 1-in/2.5-cm piece of chain and gently open the loop of an earring wire, placing the last link of chain on the loop. Open one of the jump rings and use it to connect the other end of the chain to the jewelry cap, closing the jump ring securely afterward.

3 Repeat step 2 to form your second earring.

Makes 1 pair of earrings

◠◠ GEEK SPEAK

THE CRAFT OF D&D
by Kim Mohan

When you hear "geek," do you think D&D?

If so, you're not alone. Far from it.

If not, where have you been for the last thirty years?

Dungeons & Dragons, the quintessential fantasy role-playing game, has been around longer than most of us geeks have been alive. Ever since the late 1970s, D&D has stoked the imaginations of people who want more out of a game than a couple of hours of moving a token around on a board. From its humble and crude beginnings, it has evolved into a crafty hobby that brings friends together on a cooperative quest to save the world (or at least some imaginary version of it).

You can play the game with nothing more than the rulebooks and some notepaper, or you can go the whole route, enhancing your play experience with a host of accessories. You can buy add-ons or you can make your own.

The best way to bring the game to life at the table is by using miniature figures to represent the positions of characters and monsters. "Minis" have been a hallmark of D&D play since the early days, when the figures were cast in metal and spruced up by painting them. If you have a steady hand and a really small brush, you can personalize your minis to look just the way you want them. Nowadays, though, most of the minis on the market are prepainted figures made of plastic — each a work of art in its own right.

If you have a penchant for typography or graphic design, you can design your own character sheet (the document that summarizes the characteristics and abilities of a character or creature in the game). Make customized versions for each of your friends' characters, too, and you'll earn their undying gratitude.

The action in each episode of the game happens somewhere — maybe a room in a wizard's tower replete with furnishings, maybe an enchanted forest, maybe a maze of dark dungeon corridors with monsters waiting around every bend. If you enjoy making maps and indulging your latent talent as an interior designer, you can have a lot of fun before the game even starts by laying out the places where the adventuring takes place.

Of course, no set of D&D accoutrements is complete without a bunch of dice, and you need a place to store them when you're not playing. Making your own dice bag is a pretty simple crafty activity that adds your unique personal touch to your "stuff": Start with a piece of fabric or leather that you like, stitch it up to form a pouch, stitch a lip along the top to hold a drawstring, and you've got a one-of-a-kind accessory that marks you as a true D&D aficionado.

Most of the craftwork that goes along with playing D&D is designed to help you and your friends visualize what's going on as your adventuring unfolds. Even though the action of a D&D game takes place essentially in your imagination, nothing says you can't give that thought process a little help.

KIM MOHAN *is the managing editor for Role-playing D&D at Wizards of the Coast, the Seattle company that publishes the Dungeons & Dragons game. Since entering the world of D&D as the editor of* Dragon *magazine in 1979, he has edited or written a few million words' worth of game material. He has also contributed to the Star Wars role-playing game and served as the editor of* Amazing Stories *for several years. Sure beats working for a living.*

BEST GEEKY MEMORY: *I once went to dinner at legendary science-fiction author Robert Silverberg's house. Yes, I was invited.*

A TRIO OF TRIBBLES

BY LINDA PERMANN

Every geek remembers these rapidly multiplying creatures from Star Trek, and now you can use that furry yarn at the bottom of your stash to crochet your own. This pattern is super simple to make and quick to work, so you too won't be able to stop at just one. But be sure to read through the tips on working with fuzzy yarn so that this trio of tribbles won't, well, give you any trouble! And remember—keep them away from Klingons!

Gauge is not critical to this project; just be sure that your stitches aren't so loose that you can poke your fingers through them, or the stuffing may come out. The finished purr-inducing critter measures approximately 16 in/40.5 cm in circumference (or about 5½ in/14 cm in diameter, depending on your take on tribbles!).

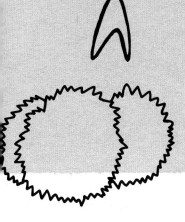

YOU'LL NEED

Tools

- Size J-10 (6 mm) crochet hook
- Row counter, or scratch paper
- Yarn needle

Materials

- 60 yd/55 m eyelash yarn
- 60 yd/55 m worsted-weight (CYCA 4) wool or acrylic yarn (Or rather than combining, just use 60 yd/55 m bulky [CYCA 5] yarn with a fuzzy texture)
- Polyester fiberfill such as Poly-fil

Stitch Key (see Glossary, page 146)

- ch = chain
- dc = double crochet
- hdc = half-double crochet
- sc = single crochet
- sl st = slip stitch
- st(s) = stitch(es)

INSTRUCTIONS

Using this master pattern, make the three tribbles shown in the photo by using the yarn combinations detailed in the section that follows. Or feel free to create your own mixes with similar yarns.

1 Holding eyelash yarn and worsted weight yarn together as one strand throughout OR using bulky yarn, ch 21.

Row 1: Ch 1, sl st in first ch, sc in next 2 ch, hdc in next 3 ch, dc in next 8 ch, hdc in next 3 ch, sc in next 2 ch, sl st in last ch, turn—20 sts.

Row 2: Ch 1, sl st in first sl st, sc in next 2 sc, hdc in next 3 hdc, dc in next 8 dc, hdc in next 3 hdc, sc in next 2 sc, sl st in last sl st, turn—20 sts.

Rows 3 to 21: Repeat row 2—20 sts.

2 Fasten off and weave in the ends.

3 Thread the yarn needle with your chosen yarn, bring it in and out of the slip stitches on one edge of the piece, pull taut to gather into a circle, and weave in yarn ends. Repeat gathering process in slip stitches on the other side of the tribble.

4 With the right side facing you and the remaining edges aligned, use the yarn needle and yarn to whipstitch the edges together about halfway up the side. Stuff the tribble with fiberfill, then sew up the remainder of the seam the same way. Weave in the ends, fluff out the fur around the seam, and enjoy your new tribble!

The Tribbles

LIGHT BROWN TRIBBLE
Joann Sensations "Cello" (eyelash yarn) in #2 Brownish Red and Patons Classic Wool in #234 Chestnut Brown

GOLDEN BROWN TRIBBLE
Crystal Palace "Splash" in Wood Grain and Cascade Yarns "220 Wool" in #8555 Black

FURRY BROWN TRIBBLE
Joann Sensations "Angel Hair" in #4729 Brown

Makes 3 tribbles

LINDA PERMANN *is a crocheter, crafter/designer, and writer living in San Antonio, Texas. She frequently contributes patterns to* Crochet Today *and* Interweave Crochet, *and is the author of* Crochet Adorned. *She blogs at Lindamade.com.*

BEST GEEKY MEMORY: *Playing Super Mario Bros. at a friend's house until my thumbs were red, because my parents didn't allow video games. I never did make it past those evil steps in Level 8.*

"MARVELOUS MACHINE" STEAMPUNK PENDANT

BY Diane Gilleland

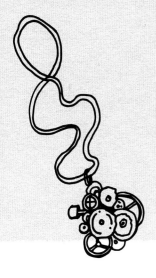

This delicate pendant is a bit like a watch turned inside out. The gears are layered on the outside to resemble a fantastical little Victorian-meets-postmodern steampunk machine. You can find watch movements and watch parts on eBay—in fact, if you use "steampunk" as your search term, you can usually find all kinds of interesting jewelry components.

Keep in mind that the parts from a lady's watch will be much smaller than the parts from a man's watch. You may need to handle some of them with tweezers.

YOU'LL NEED

Tools

- Wire cutters
- Industrial-strength or jewelry glue such as DAP or E-6000
- Toothpick
- Tweezers or needle-nose pliers

Materials

- Assorted watch gears
- 1 watch movement, without face
- Flat-backed pendant bail (see Glossary, page 148)
- Necklace chain of your choice

INSTRUCTIONS

1 Sort through your watch gears until you have a selection of thin, open gears and a selection of thicker, solid gears.

2 The open gears may have tiny spindles through their centers—if so, you can cut these off with wire cutters. Use caution if you do and be sure to wear eye protection; tiny pieces of metal can be dangerous to cut.

3 Pour out a little of the glue onto a clean work surface and, using the toothpick, pick up a tiny amount of glue. Begin gluing gears to the surface of the watch movement using the tweezers or pliers, working with just a few at a time and letting the glue set for about 10 minutes before adding more.

4 Wherever you can, glue one of the solid gears over the tops of the open gears. This will help adhere the gears more securely to the pendant.

5 When you have as many gears as you like in place, let dry for 2 or 3 hours.

6 Glue the pendant bail to the back of the movement. Let dry overnight, then add the chain—it's ready to wear!

Makes 1 pendant necklace

DIANE GILLELAND *is the author of* Kanzashi in Bloom, Making a Great Blog, *and* Social Media for Your Crafty Business. *She has contributed projects to* CRAFT, Sew News, CraftStylish.com, *and* Whipup.net. *She is also the writer and producer of Craftypod.com, a blog and biweekly podcast about making stuff. She lives in Portland, Oregon.*

BEST GEEKY MEMORY: *My favorite Halloween costume ever was the year when, at age twelve, I dressed as Princess Leia. My Mom made me a flowing white gown, complete with a belt, and I spent hours wrapping my long hair into those big head-Danishes. I even borrowed my younger brother's toy lightsaber (and let me tell you, that required a whole lot of fighting). Boy, did I think I was cool! In fact, I've rarely felt that cool since.*

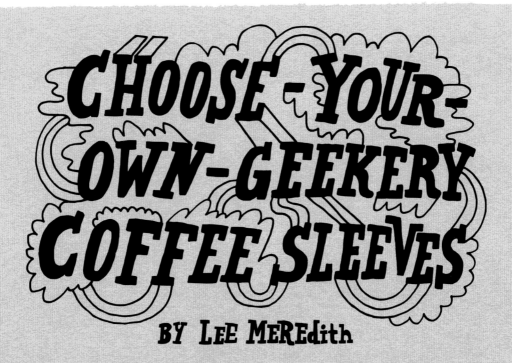

CHOOSE-YOUR-OWN-GEEKERY COFFEE SLEEVES

BY LEE MEREdith

These coffee cup sleeves are a perfect blank canvas for any type of nerdiness you can think up! They're knit from the top down on double-pointed needles, and the slip-stitch sections not only create a little extra thickness for grip and insulation for hot drinks, they also allow for colorwork that looks like Fair Isle knitting but is much easier to execute.

The instructions here begin with the master pattern for the coffee sleeve. In the section that follows you'll find the details for the three sleeve themes shown in the photo. Or you can adapt the pattern for any color schemes and themes you like.

Once the sleeve is knitted, add geek-tastic embellishments by any means and media—embroidery, appliqué, buttons, or beads. The sleeves shown here have embroidery (the Trivial Pursuit pie) and felt appliqués (the Dr. Mario sleeve).

YOU'LL NEED

Tools

- 5 double-pointed knitting needles, size US 6 or US 8 (see Sizes and Gauge, below)
- Yarn needle

Materials

- 30 to 40 yd/27.5 to 36.5 m worsted weight yarn (see Choose-Your-Own Variations, opposite page)
- Embellishment materials of your choice (I used red, yellow, and blue felt and matching threads for one sleeve and for another, embroidered with the same wools used to knit it)

Sizes and Gauge

- Smaller size (fits paper coffee cups)—Knit on size US 6 needles for a gauge of 5 stitches per inch.
- Larger size (fits bigger paper cups or iced coffee cups)—Knit on size US 8 needles for a gauge of 4½ stitches per inch.

Stitch Key (see Glossary, page 148)

- k1 = knit 1 stitch
- k2tog = knit 2 stitches together (decrease 1)
- sl1 = slip 1 stitch purl-wise

INSTRUCTIONS

1 Cast on 48 stitches, 12 on each of 4 double-pointed needles.

Row 1: Knit 1 row.
Row 2: Purl 1 row.
Row 3: Knit 1 row.
Row 4: [k1, sl1] for 1 row.
Row 5: Knit 1 row.
Row 6: [sl1, k1] for 1 row.
Row 7: Knit 1 row.
Row 8: [k1, sl1] for 1 row.
Row 9: Knit 1 row.
Row 10: [Knit to last 2 stitches on the needle, k2tog] for each needle.
Rows 11 to 26: Repeat rows 3 to 10 two more times.
Row 27: Knit 1 row.
Row 28: Purl 1 row.
Row 29: Knit 1 row.

2 Bind off. Weave in the ends with your yarn needle.

3 Add whatever nerdy embellishments your heart desires!

Choose-Your-Own Variations

FIREFLY SLEEVE

To make the sleeve inspired by Jayne's hat from *Firefly*, start with yellow yarn. Switch to orange on row 11 and switch to red on row 19. Changing colors in the stockinette stitch sections makes for smooth stripes; if you switch colors during the slip-stitch pattern parts, the stripes will be choppy.

TRIVIAL PURSUIT SLEEVE

This sleeve uses colors in the slip-stitch rows to create a Fair Isle colorwork look without the trouble of stranded knitting. Simply work slip-stitch rows 4, 6, 8, 20, 22, and 24 in the contrasting colors of the Trivial Pursuit game on a solid navy blue base. Use the same colored wool yarns to embroider a TP game pie onto the finished sleeve.

DR. MARIO SLEEVE

To make a Dr. Mario–themed sleeve, knit in solid black yarn, then add felt appliqués to create the look of the screen mid-game: cut "half-pills" in red, blue, and yellow felt, then hand-stitch to the sleeve using matching thread.

Makes 1 coffee sleeve . . . or 2, or 3 . . . depending on how much coffee you've had!

LEE MEREDITH *designs knit accessories, spins yarn, writes craft tutorials, and does whatever other creative projects come her way. She's contributed to CRAFT, CraftStylish.com, Threadbanger.com, and other crafty Web sites and books, and keeps her own blog (called Do Stuff!) at Leethal.net. She lives in Portland, Oregon, with her partner, Pete.*

BEST GEEKY MEMORY: *My early geek memories are all about Nintendo. My favorite games were the first Super Mario Bros., Super Mario Bros. 3, and California Games. Nowadays, I still love original Nintendo, but my number one favorite game is Dr. Mario!*

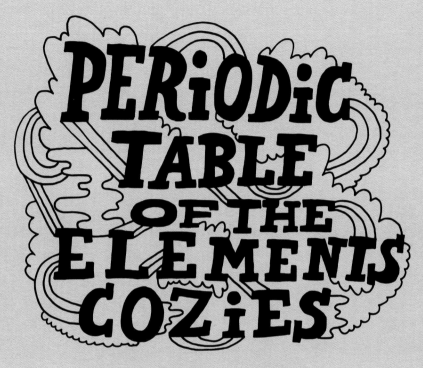

PERIODIC TABLE OF THE ELEMENTS COZIES

BY ERIKA KERN

Protect your gadgets while showing love for your favorite element with this chem class cozy. Adapt the cozy to fit your phone, iPod, camera, or anything else you can't live without. As a bonus, you'll never forget your atomic numbers again!

YOU'LL NEED

Tools

- Photocopier
- Tape measure
- Rotary cutter and self-healing cutting mat
- Iron-on transfer pen or transfer pencil (I prefer the Sulky iron-on transfer pen)
- Iron
- Embroidery needle
- Scissors
- Straight pins

Materials

- The gadget you'd like to put in the case
- Felt in 2 contrasting colors (I used a wool blend felt)
- Elements templates (in Patterns and Templates)
- Embroidery floss in any color(s) you like

INSTRUCTIONS

1 Begin by measuring your gadget. The length of the felt pieces needs to be 2 times the length of your gadget, plus the depth. The width of the felt pieces should be the width of your gadget, plus the depth, plus ½ in/12 mm for the seam allowance.

2 Once you have the measurements, use them to cut 2 pieces of felt with the rotary cutter, 1 from each color. One of the felt pieces is for the exterior and the other is for the lining.

3 To make the embroidery pattern, photocopy the Elements templates. Turn the page over and trace your chosen element on the back with the transfer pen or pencil to get the mirror image. If you're using the pen, let your ink dry fully before transferring the image.

4 Next, transfer your embroidery pattern onto the piece of felt you have decided on for the exterior. Turn off the steam and set your iron to the highest setting for your fabric (wool felt can take a linen setting, acrylic felt can't take higher than a wool setting). Warm up your fabric with a few passes of the iron (I also like to fold and press the fabric in half so that I can see where I need to place my pattern). When the fabric is warm to the touch, place the pattern on it, ink side down. Using the hot iron, transfer the image. Hold the transfer with your fingertips to anchor it as you press.

5 When your image is transferred, begin embroidering the element's details. The finished cozy pictured here used 2 strands of floss and a split stitch (see Glossary, page 147) for the element name and weight, 4 strands of floss and a stem stitch for the element abbreviation, and 4 strands of floss and a split stitch for the atomic number.

6 After you've finished the embroidery, press the front of your cozy. Place the embroidered exterior felt onto the lining felt and fold them in half vertically. Pin your sides together, leaving a ½-in/12-mm seam allowance.

7 Sew up the sides and the top and bottom layer of top opening using a blanket stitch (see Glossary, page 146).

8 Slip in your gadget and have fun!

Makes 1 gadget cozy

ERIKA KERN *has been crafting since she was old enough to hold a needle. In 2005 she started the Web site Myimaginaryboyfriend.com, where she sells her handmade wares and blogs about crafts, life, her obsession with pop culture, and her undying love of sci-fi. Her work has been seen in several magazines and on the Web site Craftstylish.com. She lives in Bakersfield, California.*

BEST GEEKY MEMORY: *Seeing* Wrath of Khan *with my parents when I was six or seven years old. I didn't quite understand what happened to Spock when he went into the radiation-filled chamber. Why did he die? After the movie I asked my mom, "Why would getting peanut butter all over him kill Spock?"*

ᴗᴗ GEEK SPEAK

COSTUMING
by Ruth Suehle

For some people, costuming is a quick stop on October 30 at the local Halloween shop to see what's left. For others, it's a year-round fascination, whether they're re-creating images from pop culture or inventing their own designs.

Costuming is especially popular among the geek set that frequents sci-fi, fantasy, and related conventions, and most such events have at least one costume contest. At some cons, costuming is so common that you'll feel more out of place in street clothes than dressed up. Some costumers also go beyond mere dress-up — they really take on the personas of their characters. The term "cosplay," a portmanteau of "costume" and "role play," originally referred mainly to anime and manga characters, but it is starting to be applied more and more often to costumers in every genre.

Making your own costumes isn't just about sewing: it's the perfect way to show off the range and variety of your crafty talents, as well as an entree to learning new ones. For one costume I created (a Pirate King costume from *Pirates of the Caribbean: At World's End*), I not only sewed the coat and pants, I had to do leatherwork, sculpting, painting, embroidery, and Chinese knot work. For other costumes, I've found myself learning about eighteenth-century underwear, how to work with feathers, and the magic that is possible when you use the right types of interfacing.

Costuming is also an opportunity to be creative with materials, unless you want to spend nearly unlimited time and money on every project. (And mind you, that's a likely enough happenstance — I once saw a Chewbacca costumer who, disappointed at the options in fur fabric, latch-hooked all of the fur onto that seven-foot-tall body by hand.)

My Pirate King and Red Queen for Tim Burton's *Alice in Wonderland* each cost less than $100 to put together. It sounds impossible, but with enough time, fabric store coupons, and sale-scouring, it can be done.

Next Halloween, try re-creating your favorite TV or movie character. Sites like Costumersguide.com and Alleycatscratch.com can help you find detailed images of the character and point you to patterns, materials, and other people who have worked on the same costume. You'll be ready for the nearest con, not to mention Best Dressed at the next Halloween party!

RUTH SUEHLE *has won several awards for costume re-creations, including Best Use of Materials for Elizabeth Swann's Pirate King costume and Best Journeyman for the Red Queen from Tim Burton's* Alice in Wonderland, *both in Dragon*Con's workmanship competition. She began cake decorating in 2004 and enjoys creating 3-D sculpted cakes. You can read about the process behind her costumes, cakes, and other creations at Hobbyhobby.wordpress.com. She lives in North Carolina.*

BEST GEEKY MEMORY: *In 2005, I was seven months pregnant with my daughter when Dragon*Con rolled around. I was disappointed at my limited costuming options, so my friend Neal and I painted Cthulhu on my large belly. A photo of it appeared in the Atlanta Journal-Constitution. Six years and several more complicated (and award-winning) costumes later, people still recognize me as "the Cthulhu belly!"*

HARRY POTTER BABY AND TODDLER COSTUME

BY Susan Beal

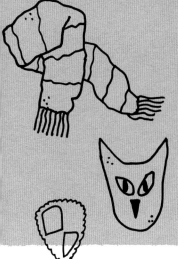

Make this quick and easy Harry Potter costume for your little one's first (or second, or third) Halloween! This project is flexible in size and length (see Note, page 85), and with luck and a moderate craft-supply stash under your belt you won't even have to make a special trip to the store. The final touch is a lip-liner lightning-bolt "scar" right on his or her forehead.

YOU'LL NEED

Tools

- Photocopier (or pen or pencil and tracing paper)
- Iron (optional)
- Scissors
- Fabric marker (optional)
- Straight pins
- Sewing machine
- Thread
- Seam ripper (optional)
- Tape measure
- Pinking shears (optional)
- Fabric glue
- Chopstick or pen (optional)
- Size US 8 knitting needles
- Yarn needle

For the robe

- Black V-neck T-shirt (see Note, page 85)
- Harry Potter Insignia template
  (in Patterns and Templates)
- Small remnants of gold felt and scarlet corduroy

For the broom

- Harry Potter Broom template
  (in Patterns and Templates)
- ¼ yd/ ¼ m dark brown felt
- 12 in/30 cm elastic, ⅜ in/1 cm wide
- 1 bag polyester fiberfill such as Poly-fil
- About 50 yd/46 m yellow bulky yarn, any type

For the scarf

- 1 skein *each* scarlet and gold worsted-weight yarn
  (I used Berroco Comfort)

For Hedwig the Owl

- Harry Potter Owl templates
  (in Patterns and Templates)
- One 8½-by-11-in/21.5-by-28-cm sheet white felt
- Scraps of amber and dark brown felt
- Cotton batting or polyester fiberfill

INSTRUCTIONS

1 **To make the robe,** iron or smooth the T-shirt flat and turn it inside out for sewing.

2 Using the diagram's dotted sewing lines as a general reference, sew to bring in the sleeves and sides of the T-shirt, keeping the lower section more flared to create the beginning of a "robe" shape. You can either use a white or light-colored fabric marker and pin or just jump in and start sewing—you can always seam-rip anything that is too tight or you don't like later, or re-stitch if it's too big.

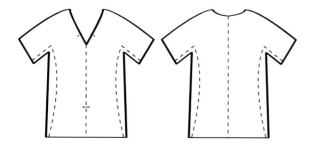

3 Continuing to work on the wrong (inside) side of the shirt and following the middle dotted lines on the diagram, sew a seam all the way down the center on both the front and the back to steal some of the wideness of the adult sizing. On the front, start sewing well above the dip of the V-neck (there's a mark on the template about one-third of the way up, where I started mine), and sew the seam together as a diagonal line, stopping about 8 in/20 cm above the bottom hem. You can always do this step in two passes if that's easier—the goal here is to make the V shorter and closer fitting instead of retaining the boxy adult shaping.

4 Keeping the robe inside out, try it on your child (or compare it to a well-fitting garment) and gather any excess material at the back so it fits nicely. Remove it from him or her and pin or hold that excess fabric in place at the back (mine was a fold of about 3 in/7.5 cm), then stitch it top to bottom. When you are pleased with the robe fit and shaping, cut the excess seams about ½ in/ 12 mm from the stitching. Also cut the front bottom section below your seam so the robe billows in the front—easier for crawling or toddling action. If it's too long, trim it with scissors—no need to hem since the fabric will roll naturally.

5 Next, photocopy or trace and cut out the Insignia templates, pin them to the gold felt and scarlet corduroy scraps, and cut out. Pink the edges of the gold shield if you like. Use the fabric glue to attach the gold base to the upper right part of the robe, and then glue the 2 scarlet quadrants over it. Let dry completely.

6 **To make the broom,** photocopy or trace and cut out the Broom template, pin it to the dark brown felt, and use it to cut 2 pieces, each 14 by 3½ in/35.5 by 9 cm. Cut a piece of elastic, about 5 in/12.5 cm long for a baby or 6 in/15 cm long for a toddler.

7 Place the 2 pieces of felt together. Double the elastic into a loop and slip it between the felt pieces, placing it where the pattern is marked "elastic loop" so just a bit of both raw edges peek out. Stitch the felt rectangles together, following the dotted lines on the pattern and leaving the bottom edge open as shown.

8 Turn the broomstick right side out, so the sewn-shut elastic loop stands out on one side, and stuff it with batting, using a chopstick or pen, if you like. Stitch the bottom closed by hand or machine—no need to make it neat and fancy, it will be covered by yarn "bristles."

9 Cut a 4- to 5-in/10- to 12-cm piece of elastic and set it aside. Cut about one hundred 18-in/46-cm strands of the yellow yarn—an easy method is to loop it around a 9-in/23-cm book or other large item, then cut one end of each of the loops. Slip the elastic through the strands of yarn at midpoint to catch them and wrap it around the broomstick about 5 in/12.5 cm above the bottom, as shown on the template, so the yarn is caught neatly around the stick. (For an older or taller child, you may want to wrap the elastic a little lower, like 3 or 4 in/7.5 or 10 cm above the bottom, to add a bit of total length.) Arrange the yarn neatly and sew the elastic in place, covering the join with a few strands of yarn.

10 Cut 1 more piece of yellow yarn 2 ft/60 cm long and wrap it horizontally around the broom "bristles," a few inches below the elastic, 4 or 5 times, knotting it securely. This is your broom!

11 *To make the scarf*, cast on 12 stitches in scarlet. Knit 18 rows. Switch to gold and repeat, switching colors every 18 rows for a total of 8 stripes. Weave in ends with a yarn needle.

12 Cast off and cut twelve 8-in/20-cm pieces of yarn in each color for fringe. Using a yarn needle or just slipping the yarn through with your fingers, add the scarlet fringe to the gold end of the scarf and the gold fringe to the scarlet end (or vice versa, if you like). Trim the ends neatly.

13 *To make Hedwig the Owl*, photocopy or trace and cut out all the Owl templates. Pin the Body template to the white felt and use it to cut 2 body pieces. Pin the Eye templates to the amber felt and use them to cut 2 eyes and 2 small circles. Pin the Beak template to the dark brown felt and cut 1 beak. Place the owl body pieces together, wrong sides in, and machine-stitch all around the edges as shown on the template, leaving a section at the bottom open for stuffing. Fill the owl with batting

and then stitch the bottom closed. Glue or hand-sew the eyes and beak in place as indicated on the template.

Makes 1 baby or toddler Harry Potter costume, including robe, broom, scarf, and owl

Note: The sizing for this project is approximate, since T-shirts, babies, and toddlers all vary wildly. For my six-month-old daughter, I used a women's size M shirt to make a robe that measured 22 in/ 56 cm long and 9 in/23 cm across at the chest. For the toddler version (approximately an eighteen-month size, give or take), we used a women's size M shirt to make a robe that measured 26 in/66 cm long and 10 in/25 cm across at the chest. A thin, tight-weave jersey is recommended over a ribbed or looser-weaved shirt. You can use a larger shirt for an older child, or size one down with wider seams in step 3—and since the fabric is stretchy, it is an easy fit for a child of any size.

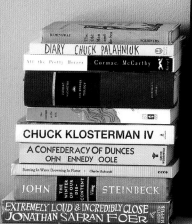

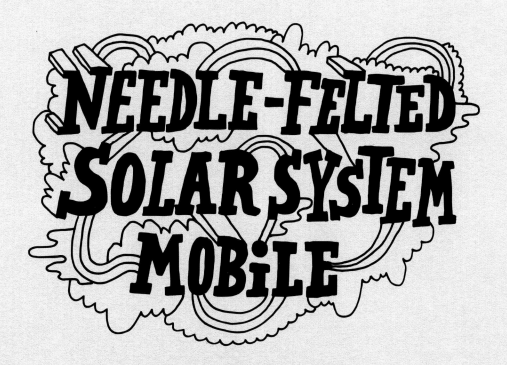

NEEDLE-FELTED SOLAR SYSTEM MOBILE

BY RacHel HoBson

Bring the simple beauty of the solar system into your home with this needle-felted mobile that's perfect for a child's room or a grown-up geek's office. The bonus of this project is that it's very forgiving and doesn't have to be precise and perfect, making it a great choice for beginners.

Needle-felting is the very addictive craft of shaping and condensing wool roving with needles to form any shape in any color you desire—and the perfect way to mix hues and add detail to a whole solar system's worth of planets.

YOU'LL NEED

Tools

- Size 36T felting needle(s)
- A needle-felting foam pad
- One 4-in/10-cm round embroidery hoop
- One 9-in/23-cm oval embroidery hoop
- One 10-in/25-cm round embroidery hoop
- Small paintbrush
- Ruler
- Scissors
- Embroidery needle
- Hook or thumbtack

Materials

- Core wool roving for the base of each planet
  (I used about 8 oz/225 g each)
- Dyed wool roving in the following colors (a sampler
  pack of roving should cover you): yellow, tan,
  charcoal, rust, gray, royal blue, green, white, light
  beige, turquoise, light blue
- 1 skein black embroidery floss
- 1 skein ecru embroidery floss
- Black acrylic craft paint

INSTRUCTIONS

1   To create the base for your first planet, pull off
a handful of the core roving and roll it into a basic round
shape. Begin poking at the shape with the felting needle
over the foam pad, paying extra attention to the placement of your fingers so as not to poke them! Continue
rotating the ball of roving around and poking until it
begins to firm into shape.

2 Continue to add layers of core roving, poking it into shape, until you have achieved almost the complete size needed. Use the photo as a reference (you may also want to find images of the planets online or in reference books for help with relative sizing). Repeat steps 1 and 2 until you have the basic shape for all of the planets and the Sun, varying their sizes from largest to smallest.

3 Using the dyed roving, add color and planetary details: again, use the photo for reference to select colors and details for each planet. Blend colors of roving to achieve gaseous atmospheres, layer roving in stripes to create striations in planets like Jupiter, and include wisps of white on Earth to create clouds. When creating Saturn's rings, roll a strand of roving between your hands to create a "snake." Felt the ring using your felting needle to compress the fibers, and shape it into a circle that will fit around your planet. Attach it to Saturn with a couple of inconspicuous stitches of embroidery floss.

4 Remove the inner ring from each embroidery hoop, and set the outer rings aside. Paint each inner ring black with acrylic craft paint and let them dry completely.

5 Nest the inner rings from smallest to largest. Attach the small circle to the oval with two 5-in/12.5-cm lengths of black embroidery floss, tied on opposite sides from one another; each embroidery floss span from the small ring to the oval should be 3 in/7.5 cm. Repeat with two more 5-in/12.5-cm lengths of black floss to attach the oval to the large circle, tying the floss on the opposite two sides of the oval, and making sure each floss span from the oval to the large ring is about 3 in/7.5 cm.

6 Hang the planets: For each planet and the Sun, thread the embroidery needle with a 3- to 4-in/7.5- to 10-cm length of ecru embroidery floss. Make a ½-in/12-mm stitch across the top of the planet, pulling the floss almost completely through. When there is about 1 in/2.5 cm of floss remaining, use both ends to tie a knot at the top of the planet. Then attach each planet to a long piece of black floss and attach that to the appropriate embroidery hoop (see step 7) by simply looping it around the hoop and tying a knot. Repeat to hang each planet. Hang the Sun from the small ring by tying a length of black embroidery floss across the diameter of the hoop and attaching the floss connected to the Sun to that floss.

7 On the oval hoop, hang Mercury, Venus, Earth, and Mars, adjusting their position to achieve the best balance possible. On the largest ring, attach Jupiter, Saturn, Neptune, Uranus, and Pluto (if you're into old-school astronomy!) and adjust their position to achieve the best balance possible.

8 Hang your mobile: Attach a length of embroidery floss to the smallest hoop, from which you will hang the mobiles. Adjust the length of the floss according to your desired hanging height. Hang using a hook or a simple thumbtack.

Makes 1 mobile

RACHEL HOBSON *is a hand-embroidery-obsessed crafter with a passion for outer space and all things geek-tastic. She writes for* CRAFT *(Craftzine.com) and maintains her personal blog, Averagejanecrafter.com, where she shares her appreciation for imperfection and promotes her philosophy that crafting is just plain fun. She lives in Austin, Texas, with her family.*

BEST GEEKY MEMORY: *My geek roots are planted firmly in my childhood love of E.T. and my adventures at Space Camp in the late 1980s. Anything related to outer space makes me giddy, and I've been known to work all day long with NASA TV playing in the background so I can listen to Mission Control chatter.*

ON-BUTTON FLAG

BY Joshua and Sarah Moon

Let everyone know that the geek is in the house by stitching up this fun flag featuring a reflective on-button symbol. Fly it proudly or simply hang it on the wall. For an easy variation, adjust the size of the flag and appliqué to make 12-by-16-in/30.5-by-40.5-cm flags, sandwich lightweight batting in the middle, and sew as directed for a set of unique place mats.

Satin or waterproof nylon fabrics are also both suitable for flag making. If you have trouble finding reflective fabric, a silver flannel–backed satin is a handy substitute. This flag is the same on both sides, but you could always create an "off" symbol for one side or come up with your own design using the instructions below as a guide.

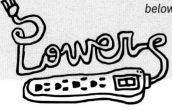

YOU'LL NEED

Tools

- Photocopier
- Scissors
- Rotary cutter and self-healing cutting mat
- Large quilting ruler
- Straight pins
- Sewing machine
- Iron
- Turning tool (optional)
- Two ⅝-in/1.5-cm grommets (optional)
- Tailor's chalk or other fabric-marking tool (optional)

Materials

- On-Button Flag template (in Patterns and Templates)
- ¾ yd/68.5 cm silver reflective fabric, 44 in/112 cm wide
- ¾ yd/68.5 cm fusible webbing
- ¾ yd/68.5 cm black cotton fabric, 44 in/112 cm wide
- ¾ yd/68.5 cm white cotton fabric, 44 in/112 cm wide
- ¾ yd/68.5 cm white cotton duck fabric, 60 in/152.5 cm wide
- Thread in colors to match fabrics

INSTRUCTIONS

1 Photocopy, following instructions for enlarging, and cut out the Flag template and pin it to the reflective fabric. Cut 2 sets of the on-button appliqué—a total of 2 circles and 2 lines.

2 Repeat with the template and the fusible webbing, again cutting 2 sets, or a total of 2 circles and 2 lines in the webbing.

3 Using your rotary cutter, mat, and quilting ruler, cut out 2 rectangles from the black cotton and 2 rectangles from the white cotton, each measuring 24 in/61 cm by 18 in/46 cm.

4 Cut a binding section measuring 26 in/66 cm by 4 in/10 cm out of the cotton duck fabric.

5 Pin together 1 black panel and 1 white panel, aligning the long sides, and sew them together, backstitching at each end. Press the seams toward the black panel.

6 Repeat step 5 with the other black and white panels.

7 Gently fold your appliqué pieces in half and press with your finger, creating a visible line in the fabric—this will help with centering the pieces on the 2 flags.

8 Center 1 set of your appliqués on each flag in classic on-button position (as shown in the photo), layering the reflective fabric over the fusible webbing—the black panels should be on the left-hand side of the flag in both cases. The straight piece of the appliqué should be centered 6 in/15 cm from the top of the flag and the bottom of the circle appliqué 6 in/15 cm from the bottom of the flag.

9 Press to adhere the appliqués, following the manufacturer's instructions on the fusible webbing packaging.

10 Set your sewing machine to a narrow zigzag stitch (or use the appliqué setting, if you prefer) and carefully stitch all the way around both pieces of appliqué on each flag.

11 Now, with right sides together (and black facing black, white facing white), pin around 3 sides of your project, leaving the left-hand (black) shorter side unpinned.

12 Using a ½-in/12-mm seam allowance and backstitching on each end, stitch around the 3 pinned sides.

13 Press your seams and clip your corners.

14 Turn the flag right side out and push out your corners using closed scissors or a turning tool. Press well.

15 Pin all around the perimeter of the flag to prevent your two layers from shifting and top-stitch ¼ in/6 mm and then ½ in/12 mm around the three sides you just sewed, stopping to change thread colors when the fabric color changes.

16 Top-stitch on either side of the center seam, from the bottom and top of the appliqué pieces in each respective color of thread.

17 To bind your flag, fold the cotton-duck binding piece in half lengthwise and press it. Open the strip and fold the long edges in toward the centerline created from your pressing. Press the binding a second time, creating a double-fold strip (like bias tape on a huge scale).

18 Pin this binding to the raw edge of the flag, so the edge is tucked inside the center crease of the binding.

19 Tuck the raw edges at the top and bottom of the binding in and around the edges of your flag and pin them into place. Stitch closed, ⅛ in/3 mm and ⅞ in/2.5 cm from the flag's edge.

20 If you want to include grommets, follow the instructions on their packaging to attach them ½ in/12 mm from the top and bottom of the flag.

21 Hang your flag using hooks, or string it up on a flagpole and let your geek flag fly!

Makes 1 flag

JOSHUA AND SARAH MOON *are a husband-and-wife team who write the blog Sewer-Sewist.com, where they chronicle the trials and tribulations of sewing, printmaking, and crafting together. They live in Portland, Oregon.*

BEST GEEKY MEMORY: *Sarah is a long-time geek, having fallen in love with all things techy in elementary school while playing Oregon Trail on an Apple IIe. A self-professed "Luddite," Josh married into the geeky way of life and has grudgingly embraced Sarah's love of gadgets—he is even known to play a few sets of Wii Tennis.*

👓 GEEK SPEAK

THE CRAFT OF SECOND LIFE
by Katin Imes

Second Life is a 3-D virtual world where over ten million users create all of the contents of the world themselves. They build cities, houses, gardens, clothes, accessories, vehicles, and even animals.

It's easy to confuse Second Life with online games like World of Warcraft, but Second Life really isn't a game; it's more of a digital canvas for creating new worlds, with a chat system added in (both voice and text chat). Many people use the worlds they create for role-playing games, classroom learning, and research or experimental simulations. Others create scenes and characters for making digital films called *machinima*. Others are finding entirely new ways to create art like comics, illustrations, and books using Second Life.

Citizens of this digital world create everything from flying dirigibles to steampunk watches, Victorian houses, medieval villages, aircraft carriers from World War II, space stations of the future, and much more. There is also the endless creation of the avatars—the digital representation of you—in this other world. For your avatar, there are clothes and hairstyles that take a skilled hand in Photoshop, as well as animations to make your avatar dance, run, fight, wave hello, or hug.

In Second Life, there is no need to stay tied to reality. Your avatar can become anything you want: a dinosaur, a bird, a zombie, a Victorian poet, a Stormtrooper, a rabbit, a dragon, a giant toaster, your favorite comic book character, or something entirely fabricated from your own imagination. There is no such thing as gravity or tensile strength, so you can build incredible structures of dreamy substance and design.

Second Life requires a new skill set that integrates and elevates a wide range of digital art tools to explore new frontiers of creation and 3-D motion art. The opportunities for creativity are virtually endless. I suggest adding it to your list of crafty things to try!

KATIN IMES *has been a computer geek since the sixth grade. He has been in Second Life since 2006, and presently owns over sixteen thousand square meters of land, where he builds new structures and meeting space both for corporate clients and for fun. He is a scripter, role player, and member of the Caledon, Isle of Wyrms, and Old Time Radio communities. He also manages an association of micro business geeks (Microbusinessoa.org).*

BEST GEEKY MEMORY: *Learning Z-80 assembly language in ninth grade—good thing I was also a choir geek, theater geek, and debate geek in high school, or else I would have been forever lost to cyberspace.*

ESSENTIAL OPERATIVE PARTS OF THE TYPEWRITER

TYPEWRITING
TECHNIQUE
COLLEGE COURSE

A Short, Easy Course for the
Development of Superior Typing Skill

By

HAROLD H. SMITH

THE GREGG PUBLISHING COMPANY
New York   Chicago   Boston   San Francisco   Toronto   London

1960

BUFFY FUSE BEAD PORTRAIT

BY SHAYNE RIOUX

Immortalize Buffy the Vampire Slayer (without turning her into a vampire) with this nearly life-sized portrait made out of fuse beads. Also known by brand names Perler and Hama, these plastic beads are laid out following a pattern on special pegboards and then simply "fused" together with a hot iron. If you'd like to make your own design, try cross-stitch design software such as PCStitch. The pegboards, available at craft stores, come in various sizes and include the ironing paper. A standard large board, like the ones called for here, are 29 beads square, or 5 beads per inch.

YOU'LL NEED

Tools

- Iron
- Ironing paper
- Wax paper
- A stack of large books, a few bricks, or anything likewise heavy you can find

Materials

- 20 large square pegboards
- Buffy pattern (page 100)
- Perler fuse beads—995 in White, 1501 in Peach, 811 in Blush, 777 in Crème, 692 in Light Brown, 1597 in Dark Brown, 17 in Hot Coral, 2129 in Black, 1807 in Dark Blue, 380 in Dark Grey, 92 in Grey
- Foam core board (optional)
- Frame of your choice

INSTRUCTIONS

1 On a large, flat work surface, lay out a row of 4 pegboards. Start laying out beads from the upper left corner of the pattern. The pattern has a grid with 10-by-10 bead blocks. (I recommend placing your beads block by block.)

2 As you continue, add more pegboards and keep placing beads until the design is complete. If you need to take a break from working on the project and want to make sure it stays undisturbed, place the sheet of foam core over it.

3 Heat an iron according to the pegboards' instructions.

4 Place the ironing paper over the first part of your design and iron in a circular motion for about 20 seconds per area. You can use the same sheet for the entire project, moving it to cover each successive section.

5 Continue until you have ironed the entire design. Check the design to make sure all the beads have been fused together.

6 While the portrait is still warm, cover it with wax paper. Stack a few large, heavy books on top to flatten out any bubbles. Set aside and let cool completely.

7 When the portrait is cool to the touch, remove the books and wax paper from the pegboards and turn the portrait over. Place the ironing paper over the backside and iron it as you did the front in step 4. When you're done, cover this side with wax paper and the books and let cool again.

8 Now you can frame and hang your portrait!

SHAYNE RIOUX *is a geek and crafter living near Washington, DC, with her husband and son (also both geeks) and way too many pets. She's been crafting for as long as she can remember. Shayne writes for the popular blog Geekcrafts.com. You can check out her crafts at Noveltykitten.com and Transcraftinental.com.*

BEST GEEKY MEMORY: *Seeing* Star Wars *on the big screen.*

Buffy Perler bead grid.

GEEK SPEAK

MIDI
by Pete Bejarano

Few combinations of different nerdy crowds have been as fruitful or had as powerful an effect on popular culture today as the combination of computer geeks and music nerds.

HISTORY
The 1970s manual-switching DIY kit-built proto-computer, the Altair, was one of the earliest affordable personal computers. The first program written for this machine by a hobbyist was a music program, which played only a few notes. Another hobbyist would write a program for that kit computer that led to the creation of a small company called Microsoft. By 1981 music companies agreed on a musical language they called MIDI: Musical Instrument Digital Interface.

WHAT IS MIDI?
MIDI is not an audio file — it is information about how to play music, which can be used to make any sound the computer or synthesizer can. Think of it as computer sheet music. Some MIDI programs and sound libraries sound amazing and are used to make the music you hear on CDs and DVDs, but other inexpensive MIDI programs sound flat or dated.

A MIDI file can have multiple tracks for multiple instruments. One could take a MIDI song meant for guitar, bass, and piano and change the track instruments to make it for flute, banjo, and tuba. MIDI captures nearly everything about a performance using 128 parameters with 128 possible values: the notes that are being played, for how long, how hard they are being hit, etc. That information is raw data that can be fed to any digital sound library.

MIDI'S REPUTATION
In the early days of MIDI (most of the eighties and the early nineties), a large segment of the population became aware of MIDI as a file format for songs they could play on their computer. The sound card the computer used, and the MIDI sound library it came with, determined how good MIDI files sounded when played back. Most mid-priced personal computers in the eighties and nineties had absolutely hideous MIDI sound libraries, and MIDI got a reputation for ridiculous (and hilarious) dated, cheesy sounds, despite the fact that MIDI is data about how to play music, and has no sound of its own.

REVENGE OF THE MIDI NERDS
Now that computers are so powerful, software exists to make MIDI data sound convincing enough to change entire industries. Over half of the music you hear while watching TV or a feature film is not string orchestra or a full band — it's some computer music nerd with a MIDI keyboard, a computer, and great-sounding MIDI-driven software. Even more music being made today in all styles, from hip-hop to heavy metal, uses MIDI — sometimes 100 percent. And those cheesy, dated sound banks that gave MIDI its reputation? They became the soundtrack to nearly every 8-bit video game we grew up with. Those simple bleeps and blips of Atari and Nintendo fame can be brought back to life with MIDI to make new music with an old-school video game feel.

PETE BEJARANO *is a music geek who works in a music store by day and co-runs a mastering studio, 1Klabs.com. He started playing piano when he was three years old, and first used MIDI to compose music at age fourteen, later getting his BA in technical theater as a sound designer. For years he was a keyboard product specialist, flying around the country training the staff of music stores about the art and science of MIDI. He lives in Portland, Oregon.*

BEST GEEKY MEMORY: *My dad played D&D in the 1970s and is a computer programmer. He used to read me* The Hobbit *and* The Lord of the Rings *trilogy before bed . . . a geeky upbringing indeed!*

WARP SPEED: *Advanced Projects*

CORALINE MYSTERY SEWING BOX

BY Susan Beal

This spooky sewing box—inspired by the wonderfully intriguing Coraline Mystery Boxes created to celebrate the movie's premiere—is full of everything a beginning sewer (or an Other Mother) could want. The cat is turned into a pincushion, a mouse into a needle sharpener, a key tag into a needlebook—and of course there are buttons galore!

Searching out vintage crafty supplies at estate sales or thrift stores will give this project a one-of-a-kind magic, but new items work just fine, too. You can also arrange your bits and Coraline pieces any way you want to, depending on the size and shape of your box.

YOU'LL NEED

Tools

- Photocopier
- Pencil
- Measuring tape
- X-acto knife
- Scissors
- Scotch tape
- Straight pins
- Sewing machine and sewing needle
- Industrial-strength glue (optional)
- Hot glue gun
- Small saw, small sharp knife, or file
- Eyelet pliers
- Fabric glue
- Thumbtack

For the box

- 1 hinged wooden box (I used a cigar box)
- One ⅜-in/1-cm sheet thick foam core
- ⅓ yd/30.5 cm red velveteen
- Coraline Pennant templates (in Patterns and Templates)
- Small scraps of ivory and olive green felt
- ½ yd/45 cm narrow white or ivory bias tape
- Thread in matching colors
- Skeleton key
- One 8½-by-11-in/21.5-by-28-cm sheet royal blue felt
- Sparkle acrylic gloss medium (optional)
- Wooden spool of thread
- Small silver stars (I found a half-yard of star trim at the fabric store and cut it apart into individual stars, but you can use fabric, paper, or any other material you like)
- Black four-hole buttons in assorted sizes (I used a total of 26)
- Black twine

For the needlebook

- Key Tag Needlebook template (in Patterns and Templates)
- Scraps of tan felt
- Eyelet
- Kitchen twine
- One ½-in/12-mm black button
- Needle threader
- Assorted sewing needles

For the pincushion

- Cat Pincushion templates (in Patterns and Templates)
- Scraps of black, royal blue, and pale pink felt
- Polyester fiberfill such as Poly-fil

For the needle sharpener

- Mouse Needle Sharpener template (in Patterns and Templates)
- Small scraps of tan and pale pink felt
- Superfine steel wool
- Two ⅜-in/1-cm black buttons

For the measuring tape and box contents

- Wooden spool of thread
- 2 large black buttons, about the size of a quarter or so
- Small tin, with or without lining (I lined mine with olive green felt)
- Vintage or new measuring tape
- Small jar lid (I used an old spice jar lid to coil the tape into)
- Small child-safe scissors

INSTRUCTIONS

1   *To make and decorate the box*, measure the inside of your box and lid, and use the X-acto knife to cut out 2 panels of foam core that are slightly smaller than the box's dimensions. (The interior sections of my cigar box measured 8¼ by 7 in/21 by 18 cm, and I marked and cut my foam core to 8 by 6¾ in/20 by 17 cm, exactly ¼ in/6 mm smaller.)

2   Cut 2 pieces of the red velveteen at least 1 in/2.5 cm larger than your foam core on each side (mine measured 10 by 11 in/25 by 28 cm). Place each piece of velveteen over a piece of foam core, fold the edges down on all sides, pulling them taut, and tape them underneath. Clip the corners if they're bulky. Test to see if the foam core pieces fit into the lid and box cavities neatly, untaping the fabric and trimming the foam core sides if they're too big. Set them aside for now.

3   Photocopy or trace and cut out the 2 Pennant templates and use them to cut out 7 pennant shapes in ivory and olive green felt (I cut out 4 in olive green and 3 in ivory). Cut a piece of the bias tape that's at least 3 in/7.5 cm longer than your lining section measures horizontally, fold it in half lengthwise, and pin the felt triangles, alternating colors, next to one another within the bias tape fold, leaving at least 1½ in/4 cm on each end open. Sew the bias tape to catch the pennants. (I used a zigzag stitch on my sewing machine, but you can stitch by hand if you prefer.)

4   Now place the skeleton key and pennant strand on the red velveteen lid liner (with raw edges of the pennant extending over each side), and arrange them as you like. Pin the pennant strand ends down at each side. Thread a sharp needle in a neutral or matching color and stitch from back to front of the foam core, taping your knot

down instead of pulling the thread. Stitch through the foam core 2 or 3 times on each end of the pennant strand to secure it. Then securely tape the thread and the ends of the pennant to the back of the foam core.

5   Stitch the key into place the same way, bringing the needle from back to front of the foam core, and sewing the key down in several places. Tape the thread ends to the back of the foam core as you did with the pennant stitching.

6   Press the lid lining, with pennant and key attached, into the box lid cavity, and then press the undecorated box lining into the box cavity—you can attach them to the box with industrial-strength glue if you like, but if the fit is good they should stay in place without it.

7   Cut a panel of the blue felt for the top of the box to the size of your choice (mine was 4 by 6 in/10 by 15 cm). If you like, apply sparkle acrylic gloss medium for a glittery effect and let dry completely. Then glue the felt down to the top of the box using a hot glue gun or industrial-strength glue.

8   Arrange your spool of thread in the center of the felt rectangle, and choose which side will face up. Mark the top and bottom ridges on one side of the wooden spool with identical straight lines. Using the saw or knife, carefully cut away the rounded parts outside the lines on the spool so that it will lie flat when you set it on its side. (If your spool is small enough, you may be able to file it down instead of sawing or cutting it.) Hot-glue the spool to the center of the felt, catching the thread tail on the underside.

9   Hot-glue the silver stars onto the felt all around the spool, Coraline-sweater-style.

10 Now arrange the black buttons all around the perimeter of the box to frame the felt square. (I varied the button sizes for a random effect.) When you are happy with the button placement, pick the first one up and thread black twine through each of the holes to "sew" an X shape on the button. Knot the twine on the back and set the button back into place.

11 Continue X-ing your buttons until you've finished them all, then attach each one to the box with a generous dab of hot glue, pushing the back knot into the glue so that the button lies flat. They'll be elevated.

12 *To make the needlebook*, photocopy or trace and cut out the Needlebook template. Pin it to the tan felt and cut out 1 key tag. Repeat to make a second tag. Pin the 2 pieces together and topstitch all around the edges, leaving a ⅛-in/3-mm seam allowance.

13 Using the eyelet pliers, attach an eyelet near the narrower end as shown in the photo and slip a piece of the kitchen twine through it to complete the tag effect.

14 Glue the black button to the circular part of the needle threader and let dry. Use the thumbtack to pierce a small hole in the needle threader, at the top of the circular area. Slip the twine through the hole, knotting it securely to join the needle threader to the needlebook.

15 Add as many needles as you like to the tag (I added 5 to mine).

16 *To make the pincushion*, photocopy or trace and cut out the Pincushion templates and use them to cut 2 cat heads and 2 pupil shapes in black felt; 2 cat eyes in blue felt; and 1 triangle nose in pink felt.

17 Use fabric glue to attach the pupils to the eyes, and the eyes and nose to the front of 1 cat head piece, as shown on the template. Let dry completely. Pin the 2 cat head pieces together.

18 Topstitch all around the edge, leaving a ⅛-in/3-mm seam allowance and leaving the bottom one-third of the cat head open for stuffing. Add fiberfill and pin the opening closed again, topstitching that section securely, too.

19 *To make the needle sharpener*, photocopy or trace and cut out the Needle sharpener templates and use them to cut out 2 mouse heads and 2 outer ears in tan felt, and 2 inner ears and 1 triangle nose in pale pink felt. Use fabric glue to attach the nose to the mouse head and the inner ears to the outer ears, as shown on the template. Let dry completely.

20 Pin the front and back mouse head pieces together, catching the layered mouse ears on each side as shown on the template. Topstitch all around the edge, leaving a ⅛-in/3-mm seam allowance and leaving the bottom one-third of the mouse head open for stuffing. Stuff the head with the superfine steel wool (this is what sharpens the needles!), and pin the opening closed again, topstitching the final section securely.

21 Hand-stitch or glue the 2⅜-in/1-cm black buttons on for the mouse's eyes.

22 *To assemble the box*, arrange the spool of thread and 2 large black buttons inside the small tin, gluing or sewing them down, or leaving them loose if you like. Coil the measuring tape into the jar lid. Arrange the needlebook, small scissors, measuring tape in its lid, thread-and-button tin, pincushion, and needle sharpener in the box as you like.

23 Sew something spooky!

Makes 1 sewing box

THE DAY THE EARTH STOOD STILL TOOLBOX

BY Paul OvErton

Embellish a utilitarian object with the ultimate in geek imagery via paper mosaic. This method can be adapted to celebrate any geeky favorites; the Gort image from The Day the Earth Stood Still *is an inspired choice!*

The method for creating paper mosaics in this project is both simple and improvisational. For quick down-and-dirty image manipulation, simply play with the images using the "posterize" filter in Photoshop. This process gives a complex image like a film and still the desired simplicity for using as a mosaic pattern.

YOU'LL NEED

Tools

- Sandpaper
- Computer with photo-editing software
- Small bowls, 1 per paper color
- Scissors
- Ruler
- Foam brush or soft paintbrush
- Tweezers

Materials

- Toolbox or other object to decorate
- Gray auto primer spray paint
- *The Day the Earth Stood Still* image to inspire your mosaic
- Transfer paper and pencil, opaque projector, or overhead projector with transparency
- Magazines or other junk paper in assorted colors
- Acrylic gloss medium such as Mod Podge Gloss

INSTRUCTIONS

1 Give the toolbox a good sanding to give it some "tooth." Spray paint the box all over with an even, thorough coat of the gray auto primer.

2 Import your image into Photoshop and use the posterize filter to render it into a high-contrast version that will lend itself well to mosaic. (For the image in the photo, I took a film still print, imported it into Photoshop, used the brightness/contrast filter to up the contrast, then posterized it using 4 tonal level, or brightness values.)

3 Next, transfer the image to the toolbox. If the image you are using is small, use transfer paper (available in many colors at fabric stores) and simply trace around the image. If the object is large, use an opaque projector or a regular overhead projector. For the latter, you will need to take a printout of your image to a copy shop and have them copy it onto a transparency. Then, using the overhead projector at home, project the image onto the surface of the toolbox and lightly trace it with a pencil. If you have an opaque projector, the transparency step can be skipped and you can place the copy (or original) on the projector and follow the same steps to trace it on with a pencil.

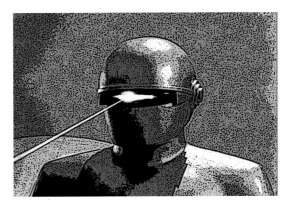

4 Once the image is on the toolbox, break out all the high-quality magazines (*Dwell* works great) and junk mail that you have lying around, and determine what your color scheme is going to be. (For my box, I used blacks, warm grays, blues, oranges, yellows, and purples.) Rip out the pages you want to use and separate them by color.

5 Set out as many small bowls as you have colors. Start cutting your mosaic pieces. (I cut the color-sorted pages into strips and then cut the strips into ½-in-by-½-in/12-mm-by-12-mm squares for an average-size project. The scale of the squares depends, of course, on the size of the project, so make bigger squares for a larger project and smaller ones for a littler one.)

6 From here, the process is both simple and, admittedly, tedious. If the project has an object in it (like the robot in this box) work that out first, starting at the edges and working toward the center (see Notes). Using the foam brush or soft paintbrush, apply a small amount of the gloss over the area where you will be laying down the "tiles." Mod Podge dries fairly quickly, so don't apply it to too large an area. Using tweezers (see Notes), begin to place tiles within the shape. When an area is finished, apply another layer of Mod Podge on top of it. Continue working until the box is covered.
That's it!

Makes 1 toolbox

Notes: The use of tweezers is key. This technique can get messy and using your fingers can damage your delicate tiles. In terms of placement and spacing, I do it all by eye, cutting and placing as I go. Surely this method takes longer, but I enjoy the improvisation of it. It's kind of like doing a jigsaw puzzle and also making the pieces. Fun!

PAUL OVERTON *is the founder of Dudecraft.com. He delights in the unusual and can usually be found in his tiny studio next to the used record shop, whipping up some sort of self-indulgent nonsense for his own amusement. Paul lives in Durham, North Carolina.*

BEST GEEKY MEMORY: *When I was eight, my dad took me to the Star Trek convention in San Francisco. I was so stoked I couldn't sleep the night before. I had visions of meeting Captain Kirk, Spock, McCoy, Sulu, and Chekov. It was a great weekend, but it turned out that we hit the autograph booth at all the wrong times. I did manage a George Takei autograph, but Shatner and Nimoy were nowhere in sight. A little disappointed, we headed toward the exit. That's when I saw Nichelle Nichols (Lt. Uhura) arrive at the autograph table. As much as an eight-year-old can have a crush, I had one on Lt. Uhura. She was very nice and was happy to sign my program. I think I said something witty and debonair like, "Uh, hi. Will you sign my program?" Clever.*

SECRET MESSAGE QUILT

BY Julie Ramsey

This striking, colorful quilt has a secret—a message in Morse code hidden in the block layout, one color per letter. For this quilt, Julie Ramsey chose a favorite Albert Einstein quote: "The most beautiful thing we can experience is the mysterious." Make her version or translate your own secret message into a quilted masterpiece!

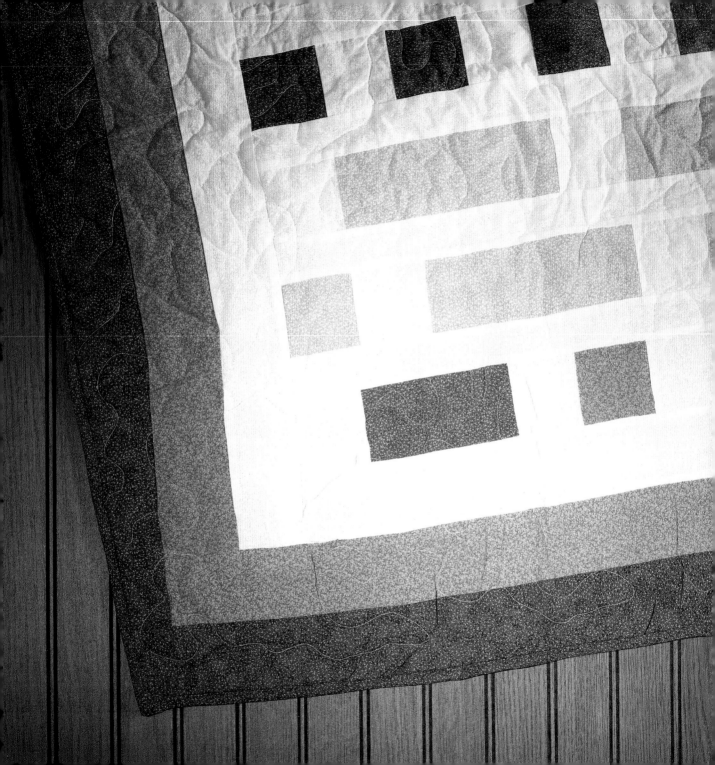

YOU'LL NEED

Tools

- Rotary cutter
- Quilt ruler
- Self healing cutting mat
- Masking tape
- Marker
- Sewing machine
- Thread
- Scissors
- Tape measure

Materials

- 1 yd/1 m *each* of 4 colors of fabric, numbered 1 to 4 (I used 1. pink, 2. blue, 3. yellow, 4. purple)
- 4 yd/3.5 m white fabric
- 1 yd/1 m *each* of 2 colors for the borders (I used blue and purple)
- Twin-size quilt batting
- 4 yd/3.5 m fabric for backing
- ½ yd/45 cm fabric for binding

INSTRUCTIONS

CUTTING, PART 1

Note: these strips are cut perpendicular to the selvedge, so they each measure 45 in/114.5 cm long.

1 Using the rotary cutter and quilt ruler, from colors 1–4, cut:
- Two 45-in/114.5-cm strips, 3 in/7.5 cm wide
- Two 45-in/114.5-cm strips, 8 in/20 cm wide

2 From the white fabric, cut:
- 23 strips, 2 in/5 cm wide
- 14 strips, 3 in/7.5 cm wide
- 8 strips, 2½ in/6 cm wide

3 From the border fabrics you've chosen, cut:
- 8 strips, 4½ in/11 cm wide

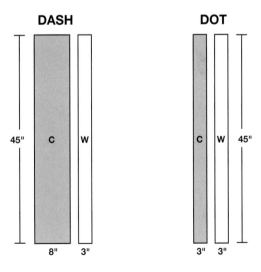

PIECING, PART 1

4 To form a dot, you'll use one 3-in/7.5-cm-wide color strip and one 3-in/7.5-cm-wide white strip. To create a dash, you'll use one 8-in/20-cm-wide color strip and one 3-in/7.5-cm-wide white strip.

1 strip of dots and 2 strips of dashes

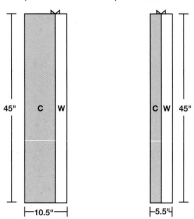

ThE MOST BeAUTiFUL THiNG WE CaN EXPERiEnCE iS THE MYSTERiOUS.

CUTTING, PART 2

5 From each of these pieces, cut 3-in/7.5-cm strips across the width of the fabric:

1. Pink
12 dots
14 dashes

2. Blue
26 dots
9 dashes

3. Yellow
20 dots
11 dashes

4. Purple
23 dots
11 dashes

PIECING, PART 2

6 Piece the rows as shown below, assembling the smaller sections end-to-end one row at a time. Spell out the message as shown:

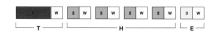

1 = ▇
2 = ▇
3 = ▢
4 = ▇

7 As you go, write the row number on a small piece of masking tape and mark the left side of the strip. This will let you assemble the rows in the correct order.

8 To assemble the horizontal sashing that goes between rows, stitch the 2-in/5-cm-wide white strips you cut earlier end to end in sets of three. Cut the double-width pieces into 2 even halves. You will need 15 of these pieces total.

9 Stitch the horizontal rows and sashing together, following the numbering on the masking tape.

10 To create the inner white border, stitch 2 of the white 2½-in/6-cm-wide strips end to end 4 times to create 4 strips 2½ in/6 cm by 88 in/2.2 m. Stitch the first and second strips to the top and bottom of the quilt, trimming the excess fabric at the ends. Then stitch the third and fourth strips to the left and right sides, also trimming the excess fabric.

To create the outer borders, stitch 2 of the blue 4½-in/11-cm-wide strips end to end 4 times to create 4 strips 4½ in/11 cm by 88 in/2.2 m for the first border. Do the same with the purple 4½-in-wide strips for the second border. Attach the first border by stitching the first and second blue strips along the top and bottom of the quilt, trimming the excess fabric at the end, and then stitching the third and fourth blue strips to the left and right sides, also trimming the excess fabric. Do the same with the purple strips to create the second border.

11 Sandwich, quilt, and bind as desired. To "sandwich" the quilt, first create the backing. Cut the backing fabric in half to create 2 pieces, each 2 yd/1.8 m long by 44 in/112 cm wide, then piece them together side by side to create a backing piece 2 yd/1.8 m by 88 in/2.2 m wide. Place the backing wrong side up and layer the batting and quilt top, right side up, on top of the backing.

Quilt as desired! (I used a large, free-motion meandering pattern. I also used the same purple fabric from my piecing to bind my quilt with mitered corners.)

Makes 1 quilt

JULIE RAMSEY *has been a quilt addict since 2003, making quilts that range from traditional log-cabin designs to one based on a game of Tetris. Julie lives in Arizona with her husband. You can follow her quilting adventures on her blog, Quiltergeek.com.*

BEST GEEKY MEMORY: *I grew up in a very geeky family, which explains a lot about the way I am now! I remember being about ten years old and joking that my dad was so smart that he could probably build a computer out of bubblegum and string. The very next evening, he taught me how to build a "computer" (a very basic boolean logic switch) using thumbtacks, paperclips, and yes, bits of string.*

LILYPAD ARDUINO CAKE

BY RutH SuEhlE

The LilyPad Arduino, designed and developed by Leah Buechley and Sparkfun Electronics, is a microcontroller board that can be sewn into clothes or other fabric creations, and can even be washed! You can attach things like motion sensors, light sensors, and LEDs to the LilyPad with conductive thread. Projects are programmed with the open source Arduino environment—find out more on the company's Web site, Arduino.cc.

The actual Arduino is about 2 in/5 cm across. This gorgeous cake, a charmingly detailed homage to the real thing, is 8 in/20 cm, and you don't have to know anything about electronics to make and enjoy it. You can find all the cake decorating items used here at baking specialty stores or well-stocked kitchen supply stores.

YOU'LL NEED

Tools

- Photocopier (or pen or pencil and tracing paper)
- Scissors
- Rolling pin
- Small paintbrush or pastry brush
- Ruler
- 2 chopsticks, 1 with square edges and 1 with round edges
- Wilton cake-decorating tips #1 and #7
- Piping (pastry) bag and coupler
- Cake-writing practice board such as Wilton (optional; see Notes, page 127)

Materials

- One 8-in/20-cm round cake (any flavor)
- 1 recipe buttercream frosting (see Notes, page 127)
- Up to 1¼ cups (to taste) of unsweetened cocoa powder
- 1 bottle each black and pink gel food coloring
- LilyPad Arduino Cake templates (in Patterns and Templates)
- About ⅓ lb/155 g Satin Ice or other purchased black fondant (see Notes, page 127)
- 1 bottle Wilton White-White or other opaque white food coloring (you'll only need a few drops)
- About ⅓ lb/155 g pale tan fondant, homemade or purchased (see Notes, page 127; if making homemade, you will also need ivory gel food coloring)
- ¼ tsp each silver and gold luster dusts
- A few drops of vodka or other clear liquor
- About ⅓ lb/155 g pink fondant, homemade or purchased (see Notes, page 127)

INSTRUCTIONS

1   Let your cake cool completely and transfer to a cake plate or serving platter.

2   Make the buttercream frosting. Transfer ½ cup/115 g of the frosting to each of 2 small bowls and set aside. Add the cocoa powder to the large bowl with the remaining 5 cups/1 lb/455 g frosting and stir until thoroughly combined and smooth. Spread the sides and top of the cake with a thick layer of the chocolate buttercream and set aside. (You may not use all the chocolate buttercream.)

3   Using the black gel 1 or 2 drops at a time, color one of the ½-cup portions of frosting pale gray. Stir until the gel is thoroughly incorporated and the color is even. Set the gray and white buttercreams aside.

4   Trace or photocopy and cut out the LilyPad Base template and set aside. Using a rolling pin, roll out the black fondant ¼ in/6 mm thick. Using the template, cut the base for the LilyPad board from the black fondant.

5   Trace or photocopy and cut out pieces #1 and #2 from the LilyPad Components templates and use them to cut 1 piece of each from the black fondant. Paint a short edge of piece #2 with the White-White food coloring, as shown on the template.

6   Gather up the scraps of the black fondant and shape a small piece into a rectangle 2¼ in/5.5 cm long by ⅜ in/1 cm wide by ⅜ in/1 cm thick. Starting just over ¼ in/6 mm from one short end, press the square chopstick crosswise into the rectangle to make a straight, shallow groove. Repeat 4 times, spacing the grooves evenly, about a generous ¼ in/6 mm apart, to create 5 grooves and 6 raised bars. Set all the black pieces aside.

7   Roll out the tan fondant to ¼ in/6 mm thick. Cut out the LilyPad Petal template and use it to cut 22 petal-shaped pieces from the tan fondant (these will go around the edges of the cake). One at a time, as soon as it is cut, shape each petal around one of the matching pieces of the black fondant LilyPad base so that they will adhere as the fondant hardens. Press the tip of the round chopstick into the center of each petal.

8   Trace or photocopy and cut out the rest of the LilyPad Components templates and use them to cut from the tan fondant: 1 piece *each* #3, #4, and #5; 2 pieces #6; 4 pieces #7; and 6 pieces *each* #8 and #9.

9   Use a side of the square chopstick to flatten the outer edges of piece #4. Indent the center so that you can place piece #5 within it.

10   In separate small bowls, mix each luster dust with a few drops of vodka. Using the prepared luster paints:
· Paint piece #4 and both pieces #6 silver and let dry. Using the chopstick, make a small lengthwise indentation in each #6 piece and insert a bit of leftover black fondant into the hollow.
· Paint piece #3, piece #5, and all the pieces #8 and #9 gold.
· Paint the outer edges of the #7 pieces silver and their centers gold.
· Place piece #5 in the center of piece #4.
· Let all the pieces dry.

11   To assemble the LilyPad, as you work, wet each fondant piece on the back before positioning so it sticks to the base. Place piece #1 in the center of the base.

12   Roll out the pink fondant and cut it into narrow strips for the pink "wiring." Each strip should be slightly narrower than ¼ in/6 mm. Experiment a few times by re-rolling and cutting.

13   Following the LilyPad Cake diagram, place the pink fondant "wires" on the LilyPad base, being sure to wet the backs as you go. Beginning with the center bottom piece (line 9), work your way across the bottom, then along the sides, and finish finally with across the top.

14   As you place the pink "wires" on the left side, also place pieces #2 through #7 as shown in the illustration on page 127.

15   As you place the pink "wires" on the right side, use the White-White icing to paint the 5 small circles and 1 square as shown on the LilyPad template.

16   To create the small pink circles (3 on the left side of the board, 4 on the right), cut a circle from the pink fondant using the Wilton tip #7 and cut out the center of that circle using the Wilton tip #1. Place the circles on the LilyPad base as shown on page 127, wetting the backs first.

17   Position the black fondant rectangle from step 6 and the gold #9 pieces, but do not place the #8 pieces yet.

18   Fit a piping bag with a coupler and the Wilton tip #1. Add the reserved white buttercream to the bag and, following the LilyPad Cake diagram, write the numbers and letters around the edge of the board. Pipe the edges of the 5 white circles and 1 white square on the right side of the board. Write "LilyPad Arduino" across the bottom of the board.

19   Clean the piping bag and #1 tip. Add the reserved gray buttercream to the bag and pipe 8 lines about ¼ in/6 mm wide on each side of piece #1, connecting to the appropriate pink "wires."

20   Carefully place the assembled LilyPad Arduino on top of the cake.

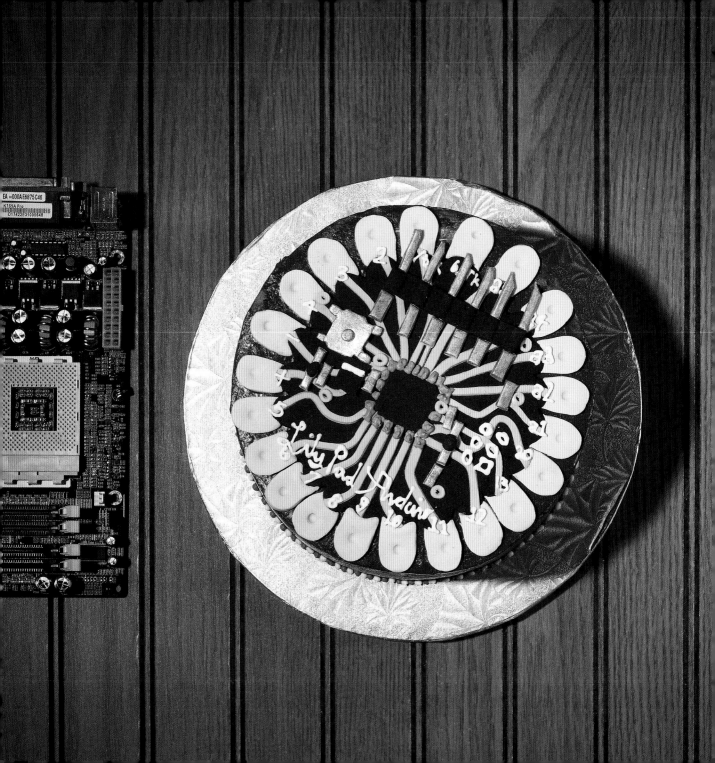

21 Following the diagram, place the #8 pieces across the top of the LilyPad.

22 Your LilyPad is complete, and ready to be admired (and eaten)!

Makes 1 LilyPad cake

Notes: ***Fondant***—You can easily make your own fondant with marshmallows and powdered sugar. The benefit to this type, commonly called marshmallow fondant (or MMF in Web forums), is that people will eat it. Store-bought fondant is often not very tasty, and most people will peel it off and throw it away. If you'd like to try it, add 2 tbsp water to 1 lb/455 g marshmallows in a microwave-safe bowl. Microwave on high for 60 seconds. Stir to help it melt, then return to the microwave for 15-second intervals until melted and smooth, stirring as needed. It will be very sticky, with the consistency of marshmallow fluff. Put 1 lb/455 g powdered sugar in a large bowl and make a well in the center. Pour the melted marshmallows into the well and mix well. Add more powdered sugar a little at a time as needed to make a non-sticky fondant you can work with. It should feel like working with children's modeling dough.

On the other hand, some decorators find marshmallow fondant more difficult to work with than store-bought. Another benefit to purchasing fondant is that you can buy it already colored; the Wilton brand has nice primary and natural colors, including pink and a light brown (i.e., tan) that will do well here. If you want to use prepared fondant but be in control of your colors, buy plain white fondant and take it from there (the Wilton Web site has great tips for how to color fondant). I strongly recommend buying the black, though; it's very difficult to get enough black coloring mixed into any type of frosting to get a true black without it starting to taste funny. Many people agree that the Satin Ice brand tastes good, and I find it really easy to work with.

Whichever route you go, you won't need much fondant—a small fist-sized ball each of black, pink, and a pale tan, or less than 1 lb/455 g of fondant total.

To color your own, use pink, ivory, and black gel food coloring (I use Wilton colors). Pat out the fondant on a clean work surface. Dip a toothpick in the gel color and spread it on the fondant. Knead the fondant to work in the color. Remember—you can always add more color, so it's better to be conservative and add more if you want it darker. Black gel makes gray fondant; a mixture of ivory and a tiny bit of black will produce a pale tan.

Buttercream frosting—Use your favorite recipe to make 6 cups/3 lb/1.4 kg, the amount you'll need to frost and decorate the cake. You'll can also find plenty of recipes online, along with extensive debate about which fat to use. I get good results with a mixture of shortening and butter using this recipe: In a large bowl, beat together 1 cup/225 g unsalted butter and 1 cup/225 g vegetable shortening. Beat in 2 tsp vanilla extract. Add 6 cups/600 g powdered sugar and beat until smooth. Add up to 2 cups/200 g more as needed to reach a spreadable but not runny consistency. (If your personal taste preferences require all butter or all shortening, that's OK, too.) *Makes 6 cups/3 lb/1.4 kg*

Piping tip—Practice piping this particular style of numbers and lettering by placing a piece of plastic wrap over the text on the LilyPad Cake template and tracing it, or by using a practice board.

For more about Ruth, see page 79.

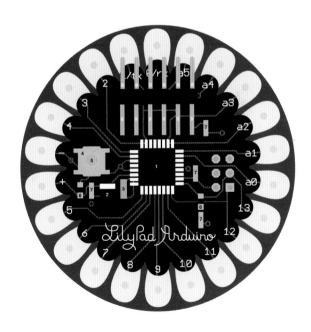

VINTAGE SCi-Fi BOOKCozY

BY ADaiHa COViNGToN

Want to protect the artwork on your favorite vintage paperbacks? Sew a one-of-a kind cozy to hold your favorite book when you take it with you on the go. You can either embroider or stencil the vintage sci-fi style robot, whichever you like. This project is adjustable to accommodate paperbacks up to about 1½ in/4 cm thick.

YOU'LL NEED

Tools

- Photocopier
- Scissors
- Straight pins
- Iron and ironing board
- Ruler
- Sewing machine, fitted with a new machine needle (the interfacing is pretty thick!)
- Needle for hand-stitching

FOR AN EMBROIDERED ROBOT

- Sulky iron-on transfer pen
- Embroidery hoop, smaller than 7 in/17 cm across
- Embroidery needle

FOR A STENCILED ROBOT

- Felt-tip marker or scanner and printer
- Self-healing cutting mat
- X-acto knife
- Small, sharp scissors (optional)
- Felt-tip fabric markers (I used FabricMate)

Materials

- Vintage Sci-Fi Book Cozy template (in Patterns and Templates)
- One 7¾-by-15-in/19.5-by-38-cm piece Pellon sew-in heavyweight interfacing
- One 7¾-by-15-in/19.5-by-38-cm piece outer fabric (I used light green linen, but you could use any light- to medium-weight fabric—solid or print!)
- One 7¾-by-15-in/19.5-by-38-cm piece lining fabric (use a cotton with a fun pattern!)
- Two 8-in/20-cm lengths rickrack or ribbon (I used two different sizes: thin rickrack for the bookmark and a wider piece to secure the adjustable flap)
- Thread in matching and coordinating colors
- A favorite paperback book, no more than 1½ in/ 4 cm thick

FOR AN EMBROIDERED ROBOT

- Robot Embroidery pattern (in Patterns and Templates)
- Six-strand embroidery floss in colors of your choice (I used orange and dark blue)

FOR A STENCILED ROBOT

- Robot Stencil pattern (in Patterns and Templates)
- Freezer paper (not wax paper)
- Scrap of fabric, about 3½ by 4 in/9 by 10 cm but no smaller (use a light color unless you are going to use an opaque paint on your stencil)
- Piece of lightweight fusible interfacing, slightly smaller than your fabric scrap
- One 4-by-4 ½-in/10-by-11-cm piece felt

Note: If you are going to embroider your robot, you need to do it before you sew the cozy. If you are going to stencil, sew the cozy first and then embellish it.

INSTRUCTIONS

EMBROIDERING YOUR ROBOT

1 If you're embroidering your robot, start with that. Find photocopy (following enlarging instructions) and cut out the Robot Embroidery pattern, and photocopy and cut out the Book Cozy template to use for reference in placing your design. Using the Sulky pen, trace the lines on the embroidery pattern. Let dry completely.

2 Center the robot design on the outer fabric, tracing side down, as shown on the Book Cozy template (about 4 in/10 cm from a short side). Pin it in place to avoid shifting while ironing. Using your iron's hottest setting without steam, press firmly; check at 15- to 30-second increments to see if the design has transferred (again, make sure the pattern doesn't shift!).

3 Once the design has transferred, insert the fabric into the embroidery hoop, pulling it taut but not so tightly that you will permanently distort your fabric.

4 Thread the embroidery needle with a manageable length of floss and embroider along the pattern lines with a backstitch (see page 147). You can outline your robot entirely in this stitch, or you can find many other decorative stitches online. Accent with French knots, cross-stitches, or other stitches you like, and feel free to switch colors in your work. Knots may be visible in your completed project, so if you use them, make them small. (I prefer to hold down a tail of floss on the back of my work, stitching over it on the back as I work.)

5 Remove your fabric from the hoop and press it, being careful not to flatten your embroidery. Now you're ready to make the cozy.

SEWING YOUR COZY

1 To sew your book cozy, you'll use the book cozy template for reference and placement. Layer the interfacing, then the outer fabric (right side up), then the lining fabric (wrong side up) and line up the sides of the rectangles. Pin the pieces together, inserting the rickrack piece you are using for your bookmark between the inner and outer fabric pieces as shown on the book cozy template. The rickrack should be completely encased in the layers except for a tail about 1 in/2.5 cm long.

2 Sew around all sides of the book cozy, using a scant ¼-in/6-mm seam allowance and leaving a 3-in/7.5-cm opening on the short side that will be the back flap (the side farthest from your bookmark), as shown on the template.

3 Turn inside out so that the right sides of both the outer and lining fabrics are showing and the interface is nestled inside. Press the cozy, turning in the seam of the opening as you do so. Hand-stitch the opening closed.

4 Fold the front flap under 1¼ in/3 cm as shown on the template and press. Hand-stitch the flap to the main cover along the top and bottom edges with coordinating thread.

5 Tuck the front cover of the paperback book into the newly created front flap, then fold the adjustable back flap over the back cover of the book. Remove the book from the cozy and press the flap. For this cozy, the adjustable flap was about 3 in/7.5 cm wide.

6 Open the flap you just pressed and pin the second rickrack piece to the inside lining fabric at the top edge, about 4¾ in/12 cm from the corner. Hand-stitch it firmly in place. Close the flap, turn the rickrack under on the opposite side of the flap, and pin it to the lining. Leave enough slack to be able to adjust the flap, but not so much that it will not hold it in place. Open the flap again and hand-stitch the rickrack in place.

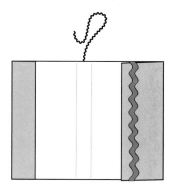

STENCILING YOUR ROBOT

1 To stencil the robot onto your finished cozy, photocopy (following enlarging instructions) and cut out the Robot Stencil pattern. If tracing, place a piece of freezer paper (larger than the image by generous margins) over the pattern with the rough, non-shiny side of the freezer paper facing up. Using the felt-tip pen, trace the pattern. If using a printer and scanner, first scan the Stencil pattern. Cut a piece of freezer paper to fit your printer (mine was smaller than a standard sheet of paper, but it worked fine; just make sure that the paper is aligned in the printer so that the design prints on it). Select the print settings so that the scanned file prints out at about 3 by 3 ½ in/7.5 by 9 cm; using the manual feed, print on the freezer paper. If you cannot size it, simply copy the pattern directly with a multifunction printer/scanner.

2 Once you have successfully traced or printed the design on the freezer paper, place the paper on the cutting mat and, using the X-acto knife, carefully cut out the white sections. Use short and steady straight lines to create curves instead of trying to make one long cut for a sharp curve. It might help to doodle on a scrap of freezer paper and practice cutting before attempting your stencil. Hold the stencil steady while cutting delicate areas to avoid tearing it. Mind the blade, though! A pair of small, sharp scissors can be helpful for tiny snags. You can omit the tiny areas like the eyes and windows, if you don't mind less detail, but they really aren't very hard to cut out: cut all parallel lines in a row, then go back and do the opposite lines, and they will be easy to remove. You will have 2 pieces to your stencil, the outer television and the inner movie part.

3 Iron the fabric scrap to remove any wrinkles and place right side up on an ironing board. Center the outer television stencil—shiny side down!—on the fabric scrap and with a hot, dry iron (I used my iron's hottest non-steam setting with no problems), press the stencil in increments of a few seconds at a time until the image is adhered to the fabric. It won't take long. Now center the movie part of the stencil inside the outer ring and, while holding down on one side to prevent it from shifting, press it with

the iron until adhered. Finally, give the entire stencil a quick press to catch anything you missed.

4 Using the fabric marker, carefully ink in the stencil, dabbing gently rather than brushing and making sure that you evenly coat all the cut-out areas. Let dry (this should only take about 5 minutes). Peel off the stencil; it should remove easily and leave no residue on your fabric. Although the instructions included with many fabric markers claim you don't need to heat-set the ink, pressing the image for a minute or so with a hot iron couldn't hurt for a fail-safe stenciled image.

5 Following the package directions, fuse the interfacing to the back of the fabric scrap. Round the corners of your piece of felt. Cut out the center to make a "frame" about ½ in/12 mm thick, rounding the corners to match. Either machine-sew or hand-stitch the inside of the frame to your stenciled fabric, centering the image in the frame. Hand-stitch (I used a slip stitch) the outside of the frame to your completed book cozy.

6 Bring your book along for your next adventure!

Makes 1 book cozy

ADAIHA COVINGTON *is a lifelong bookworm and crafter living in Oklahoma City. She collects vintage sci-fi novels and loves stories about time travel and robots. She also loves to sew, bake, and make just about anything; read about it on her blog at Adaiha.blogspot.com.*

BEST GEEKY MEMORY: *"Treating" my mom to the movies for Mother's Day by taking her to see* Teenage Mutant Ninja Turtles.

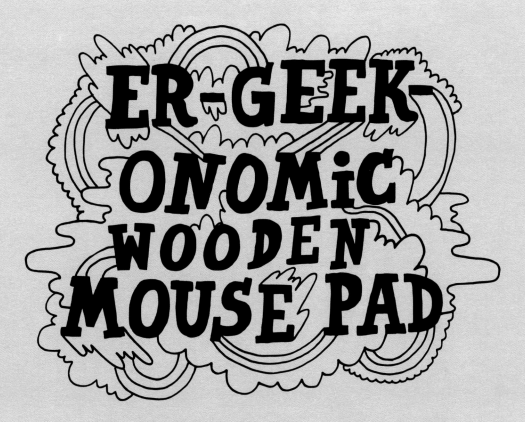

ER-GEEK-ONOMIC WOODEN MOUSE PAD

BY KAYTE TERRY and ADAM LOUIE

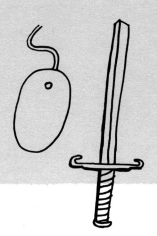

Spawned from many late nights of gaming, the wooden mouse pad hails from a time when fantasy characters needed a little augmentation, in this case, by way of ye olde mouse guidance with a wrist rest. Whether you are raiding deep into the night or fulfilling your fate as the only one who can avert the world from certain doom, the wooden mouse pad will give you the plus-one to beat the overlords and swing (or click) your way to victory.

YOU'LL NEED

Tools

- Photocopier (or pen or pencil and tracing paper)
- T-square or ruler
- Compass (preferably one that locks)
- Jigsaw
- Fine sandpaper
- Pencil
- Tracing paper
- Wood-burning tool, or black paint or permanent marker
- Eraser
- 2 fine-tipped paintbrushes
- 2 disposable mixing containers, 1 to mix the primer coat and 1 to mix the flood coat
- 4 small foam brushes
- Butane torch (optional)
- Strong needle (suitable for leatherwork), or a sewing machine fitted with a leather needle
- Thread
- Pinking shears
- Scissors
- E-6000 or other industrial-strength glue

Materials

- One 8-by-12-by-¼ in/20-by-30.5-cm-by-6-mm piece wood
- Mouse Pad template (in Patterns and Templates)
- Stain in a color of your choice (optional; a darker color will hide pencil marks, a lighter color will make colors stand out more)
- Metallic paint in two colors such as Brush 'N Leaf
- 8 oz/250 g resin such as EnviroTex Lite
- Two 8-by-2-in/20-by-5-cm pieces scrap leather
- 2 cups (10 oz/315 g) uncooked rice
- One 8-by-12-by-¼ in/20-by-30.5-cm-by-6-mm piece nonslip material, such as those used to line cupboards

INSTRUCTIONS

1 Use the ruler to find the center of the wood length and width-wise. Position the compass's point at the center and adjust the pencil leg out to meet the edges of the sides and top. Make sure the grain runs up and down the length of the wood. This will be crucial for getting a cleaner cut.

2 Use the compass to draw a half circle on the wood. Use the jigsaw to saw along the line you drew and sand out the edges and surface until everything is smooth. If you don't have a jigsaw, you can get this done at your local lumberyard or ask a handy friend.

3 You'll want to start your drawing at least 2 in/5 cm from the bottom because that's where the wrist rest is going to go. Photocopy or trace and cut out the template and use a pencil to trace the image onto a sheet of tracing paper.

4 Flip the sheet over onto your wood, traced side down, and trace over the lines, again with a pencil, to transfer the drawing.

5 Use the wood-burning tool to outline your image. If you don't have a wood-burning tool, use either black paint or a permanent marker to outline. Erase all pencil marks.

6 Stain your wood, following the manufacturer's instructions. Let dry, then lightly sand its front and sides.

7 Paint on the image, using the metallic paint and fine-tipped paintbrushes, and working slowly. Let dry.

8 In a disposable mixing container, mix the resin for the primer coat (see Note). Use one of the foam brushes to apply an even coat. Let dry.

9 When the primer has dried, in another disposable container, mix a batch of resin for the flood coat. If you have a butane torch, use it to get out the bubbles (see Note). Let the primer cure for at least 24 hours.

10 Now make the wrist rest. Using either a strong needle and thread or a sewing machine fitted with a leather needle, sew the 2 pieces of leather together, leaving a ½-in/12-mm seam allowance and 2 in/5 cm open on one long end for filling. Trim the edges with pinking shears.

11 Fill the wrist rest three-quarters full with rice and sew it closed.

12 When the mouse pad is completely dry, glue the wrist rest to the lower part of the mouse pad as seen in the photo on page 138.

13 Trace and cut the nonslip material to the size of the mouse pad. Glue the material to the bottom of the mouse pad, then let dry.

Makes 1 mouse pad

Note: Follow the manufacturer's directions for mixing resin for primer and flood coats. If you don't first put down a primer coat, the flood coat will soak into the wood and cause the finished surface to be uneven. The primer seals in and smoothes over all the inconsistencies in the wood so the flood coat can achieve the desired glassy look.

With resin, a lot of tiny bubbles, sort of like frozen versions of carbonated soda, are produced by the mixing process. You can use a small butane torch to get the bubbles out: a few minutes after pouring the resin, turn on the torch and hold it about a foot away from the mouse pad. Using a broad, sweeping motion and keeping the distance at about a foot, pass the torch across the pad. The tiny bubbles will dissipate when the heat reaches them, leaving a smooth, bubble-less surface. If you don't have a torch, the resin will still cure, but it'll have some bubbles in it.

ADAM LOUIE *is from Oregon but lives in Philadelphia with his partner Kayte. By day, Adam makes Web sites, but he likes working with his hands so by night he is a baker, crafter, and beer-maker.* **KAYTE TERRY** *is a crafter and author living in Philadelphia with Adam. She has written two books,* Complete Embellishing *and* Appliqué Your Way. *To read more about Kayte's craft adventures, visit Thisisloveforever.com.*

BEST GEEKY MEMORY: *Adam's favorite geeky memory comes from spending hours making Marathon maps with his brother then staying up too late playing crazy levels full of traps and exploding Bobs. Kayte's favorite geeky memory is meeting Adam.*

DRIVE-IN MESSENGER BAG

BY RUTH SUEHLE

The Web is full of impressive LED craft projects, including ones you can wear. Many of them use an open-source, washable microcontroller board called the LilyPad Arduino (see page 123). But if you've seen all those great LED wearables and are intimidated by things like actuators and programming, this is the project for you. Celebrate your favorite sci-fi movie scene with this fun take on the classic drive-in movie theater.

YOU'LL NEED

Tools

- Photocopier (or pen or pencil and tracing paper)
- Scissors
- Ruler
- Sewing machine
- Iron
- Freezer paper
- Paintbrush
- Straight pins (optional)

Materials

- 1 yd/1 m *each* exterior fabric and lining fabric (see Notes, page 145)
- Thread
- Drive-In Stencil templates (in Patterns and Templates)
- Black fabric paint
- Small strand of LED lights, at least 4 bulbs, in red (see Notes, page 145)
- 2 pieces Styrofoam, about ⅓ in/8 mm thick and just large enough to fit around the back of each LED (optional)
- Fabric glue (optional)
- One 3¾-by-5 ½-in/9.5-by-14-cm piece clear vinyl
- One 17-by-3-in/43-by-7.5-cm piece plastic canvas (optional)
- One 3½-by-5-in/9-by-12.5-cm printout of your favorite classic sci-fi movie scene (see Notes, page 145)

INSTRUCTIONS

1 Cut 1 body and 1 strap piece *each* from the exterior and the lining fabrics. Cut 1 interior flap piece and 1 battery compartment piece from the lining fabric only. Use the following measurements:

- Body: 21 by 40 in/53.5 by 101.5 cm
- Strap: 46 by 4 in/117 by 10 cm
- Interior flap: 2 by 6 in/5 by 15 cm
- Battery compartment: The easiest way to do this is to use the battery compartment from the LED strand you are using as a template and add ½ in/12 mm to each side for the seam allowance.

2 Holding the lining body piece vertically, fold up 13 in/33 cm from the bottom. Sew the 2 side seams with a ⅝-in/1.5-cm seam allowance. The lower section will be the bag and the upper section will be the front flap.

3 Flatten 1 corner of the bag so that the side seam lies against the bottom fold and the corner makes a triangle. Measure 1½ in/4 cm from the tip, and then sew straight across to make a 3 in/7.5 cm long seam. Repeat for the other corner. Trim the seams.

See illustration on page 144.

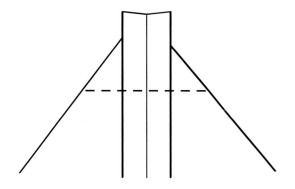

4 Make a buttonhole 4 in/10 cm long and 4½ in/11.5 cm from the top edge of the front flap. (This will provide a means to take the lights out when you need to wash the bag.)

5 Sew 3 sides of the rectangular battery box piece behind and to the right of the buttonhole, on the side opposite the bag opening. Leave the pocket open beside the buttonhole.

6 Fold the interior flap piece in half lengthwise and sew down the open long side. Turn the tube right side out and press it flat. Finish both short ends with a seam to reinforce them. Attach the flap about ¼ in/6 mm to the left of the buttonhole opening to keep it covered.

7 Follow steps 2 and 3 to sew the side seams and bottom corners of the exterior bag piece.

8 Trace or photocopy and cut out the Drive-in Stencil templates and use them to carefully cut the shapes from the freezer paper.

9 Center the freezer paper stencil, waxy side down, on the front flap of the exterior bag piece. Place the bottom edge of the tires 2 in/5 cm above the edge of the fabric. Iron the freezer paper to the flap.

10 Using the black fabric paint, paint in the exposed areas of the stencil. Be careful near the edges; dab the paint at a 90-degree angle or brush from the paper toward the fabric to be sure paint doesn't bleed under the edges. Let dry completely before peeling the stencil off.

11 Poke 4 small holes where the 4 tail lights would be (see Notes, page 145). Make the holes just large enough for the LED lights to fit through, or they'll slip out. Insert the LED. If they do slip, cut 2 slits in each piece of Styrofoam (1 piece for each car). Put the Styrofoam behind the cars, and slide the wires into the slits to hold the lights in place. You can use a little fabric glue to keep it in place, if needed.

12 Center the vinyl rectangle over the painted movie screen posts. Sew down the sides and bottom edge so that the image you're using fits snugly inside.

13 Put the right sides of the 2 strap pieces together and sew the long sides with a ⅝-in/1.5-cm seam allowance. Turn the tube right side out and iron it flat. If you'd like to shorten the strap, pin it to the bag, try it on, and cut off any excess. Leave 3 in/7.5 cm at either end for attaching to the bag. Turn the short ends inside, and top stitch all 4 sides.

14 Turn the exterior piece of the bag right side out and the lining wrong side out. Put the exterior piece inside the lining so that their right sides are together. Sew the side along the bag opening and the 2 short sides of the front flap. Leave the bottom of the flap open.

15 Turn the bag right side out through the opening you left. As you're turning the bag, insert the plastic canvas, if using, into the bottom of the bag between the lining and exterior to create a base.

16 Turn the edges of the open flap edge inside, pin down, and top stitch all 3 edges of the front flap.

17 Sew the strap right side out to the outside of the bag. The most secure way is to sew a rectangle through all the layers, then sew an X inside the rectangle from the corners. Repeat on the other side.

18 Slide your classic sci-fi movie printout into the vinyl pouch.

19 Using the buttonhole in the back of the flap, insert the lights into the headlight holes. Turn on the lights, slide the battery pack into its pocket, and let the show begin!

Makes 1 messenger bag

Notes: Make sure one of the fabrics you choose is relatively sturdy to help the bag keep its shape. For example, I chose a microsuede for the exterior, so I used a sturdier canvas for the lining.

You can find LED strands in craft stores, usually in bunches of 10 or 12. White ones are always available in the wedding aisle. For colors, you may have to order online or wait for a holiday—red ones are easy to come by at Christmastime. If the strand you buy has more lights than you need, be sure to either use fabric thick enough to keep them from showing through, or cover the extras in black electrical tape.

For your movie image, try Openflix.com, or do a Web search for "public domain movies." You can take screenshots from the films or find a still that you like online. The scene I chose is from the 1936 Flash Gordon film serial. You can get it at Doctormacro1.info.

For your tail light holes, with many fabrics, the fabric paint alone will keep it from raveling. Paint the back side around the hole edges as well. If you are using a loosely woven fabric, you can use a knitting needle to push the threads aside; making a hole this way instead of cutting the threads will keep it from raveling. (If you choose this method, it may help to mark where the lights will be before painting, since it will be difficult to poke through the paint.) Alternatively, if your sewing machine has an eyelet plate, you can use that stitch to make the hole, or you could use a hand-sewn eyelet stitch.

For more on Ruth, see page 79.

GLOSSARY

Acrylic gloss medium
A clear adhesive and topcoat, ideal for collaging or paper mosaic. It's also available in matte finish and in a sparkle version with glitter.

Acrylic spray paint
Clear spray paint that creates a strong, smooth, and durable coating. Avoid shellac-based paints for decals.

Aida fabric
Also called Aida cloth. *See* **Cross-stitch fabric.**

Appliqué
Applying an embellishment or fabric layer to a surface using sewing or another method.

Backstitch
See **Embroidery stitches.**

Bias tape
A long, double-folded strip of fabric usually used for finishing, edging, or binding a project—the raw edges of a piece of fabric, or several layers, can be tucked inside and then sewed securely in place. Also called binding.

Binding off
The final step in a knitting project, the process of knitting or purling while slipping the finished stitches over one another to give your last row of open stitches a neat, finished edge.

Blanket stitch
A hand-sewing technique for finishing the raw edge of a blanket or other project.

Bulky yarn
A thick yarn used for dense or heavy knitting or crochet, also called "chunky"; these yarns are designated with a 5 in the CYCA system.

Buttercream
A dense frosting generally made with butter or shortening and sugar, ideal for a smooth base layer of any color.

Casting on
The first step in any knitting project: the process of adding loops of yarn to your needles onto which you can then knit and purl.

Clasp
A jewelry finding used to securely close a necklace or bracelet; common types include hook and lobster.

Craft glue
A good general glue for most materials, usually nontoxic. It's best for stationary items that won't bear weight or get wet.

Craft wire
An inexpensive, pliable wire for jewelry making or other crafts that comes in assorted gauges—the larger the number, the smaller the wire's diameter, and vice versa.

Crochet stitches
Chain crochet—Yarn over and draw the loop through the loop on your hook.
Double crochet—Yarn over and insert the hook into a stitch, then yarn over again and draw the loop through the 2 loops on your hook.
Half-double crochet—Yarn over and insert the hook in a stitch; yarn over and draw the loop through the stitch; then yarn over again and draw the loop through all 3 loops on your hooks.
Single crochet—Insert the hook into a stitch, yarn over, and draw the loop through the stitch; yarn over again and draw the loop through the 2 loops on your hook.
Slip stitch—Insert your hook into a stitch, yarn over, and draw the loop through the stitch and loop on your hook.

Cross-stitch
Two running stitches that cross at their centers to form a neat X, ideal to use with woven cross-stitch fabric or as part of an embroidery pattern.

Cross-stitch fabric
A special loose-weave fabric available in a variety of scales, perfect for cross-stitching or any gridded design.

Decrease
A knitting technique to reduce the number of stitches on your needles.

Double-pointed needles
Knitting needles with two pointed ends (instead of one pointed end and one stopper), ideal for knitting something of small diameter like a sock or a coffee cozy.

Embroidery floss
Brightly colored thread for embroidering or other decorative stitching, usually in a six-strand configuration. Each brand uses codes for consistent color, which you can use to match other work and photos you see. Our book uses DMC brand color codes.

Embroidery stitches
Backstitch—A very useful embroidery stitch that creates a durable join while leaving a neat line. It shows as a continuous set of stitches on the right side of the fabric, and shows the reinforced "back" stitches on the wrong side. Also used in sewing.
Cross-stitch— Two running stitches that cross to form a neat X, ideal to use with woven cross-stitch fabric or as part of an embroidery pattern.
Split stitch—A variation on the backstitch, the split stitch is formed by piercing each previous stitch with your needle, "splitting" them to move into the next stitch.
Stem stitch—Another variation on the backstitch, the stem stitch overlaps each previous stitch slightly to one side, forming a slightly twisted line that is ideal for outlining or more organic details.
French knot—A decorative stitch made by looping the embroidery floss around your needle several times before inserting it back into the fabric, very close to the original stitch.

Eyelash yarn
A single-strand novelty yarn with a feathery fringe of "lashes," usually used for embellishments or accents.

Fabric glue
A durable glue specially designed for joining layers of fabric together or adding an embellishment to clothing or other fabric items. It's often machine-washable or dry-cleanable—check the label.

Fabric scissors
Sharp scissors for cutting fabric smoothly—to keep them in good crafty condition, do not use them for paper or other cutting.

Felt
A thick and opaque fabric made of acrylic, wool, or a blend of materials that does not fray.

Felting needles
Sharp, precise, hand-held needles used to manipulate, shape, and condense wool roving. *See* **Wool roving.**

Fondant
A smooth, thick, moldable icing that can be shaped into elaborate designs on a cake. It's easy to make your own with marshmallows and powdered sugar; there are also good-quality commercial fondants available.

Freezer-paper stenciling
This technique involves cutting a design out of freezer paper, ironing the outline (the negative) to the surface you want to stencil onto for a temporary bond, and painting the exposed area to create a perfect replica of your design. You can often use a freezer paper stencil twice if you are careful with it, but it usually isn't ideal for multiple uses beyond that.

Fuse beads
Also called by their brand names Perler or Hama, fuse beads are small, colorful plastic stock specially made to be arranged in mosaic-style designs on reusable pegboards, then heat-fixed with an iron and removed from the board. The beads, pegboards, ironing paper, and patterns are available at well-stocked craft stores.

Gauge

The number of stitches and rows per inch in knitting, also known as tension. When starting out with a new or unfamiliar knitting pattern or yarn, it's best to first knit a "gauge swatch" to test how the gauge is working.

Industrial-strength glue

A strong and durable multipurpose glue that is ideal for heavy or weight-bearing projects. Be sure to work in a well-ventilated space when using these often very toxic glues.

Interfacing

A thick, fusible or sew-in layer to add stiffness and body to a fabric project. Also called webbing.

Jewelry glue

A light but strong clear glue ideal for joining metal, glass, acrylic, or other jewelry elements. Be sure to work in a well-ventilated space when using these often very toxic glues.

Jewelry findings

Components like clasps, bead caps, and earring wires that connect and finish a piece of jewelry.

Jump ring

A circle of wire with an opening, ideal for joining clasps to chains or other jewelry components. It can be securely opened and closed with pliers.

Knitting stitches

Slip stitch—Transfer a stitch from one needle to the next without knitting it.
Stockinette stitch—A knitting pattern in which the first row of stitches are knitted, the second purled, and so on, making one side of your finished knitting smooth and one bumpy.

LED (light-emitting diode)

These efficient, long-lived, shock-resistant, fast-switching, and bright semiconductor light sources come in miniature sizes perfect for programming in craft projects.

Paper mosaic

Creating a design by arranging "tiles" of cut paper on a painted, metal, or wooden surface.

Pendant bail

A jewelry finding that converts any flat-backed piece into a pendant suitable for hanging on a chain.

Piecing

Joining pieces of fabric together with narrow (usually ¼-in/6-mm) seams to create a quilt block or quilt top.

Pinking shears

Scissors with special jagged blades that cut fabric with a neat and decorative zigzag edge, making it less likely to fray.

Pliers

Hand-held tools ideal for working with wire and many other craft materials. Pliers come in several common types: flat-nosed for bending at angles or gripping, round-nosed for forming loops and curves, and wire cutters for clipping, among others.

Plain loop

A simple circle at the end of a piece of wire, formed with round-nosed pliers, that can easily join with another plain loop to connect beads or other decorative elements, or with a clasp or other jewelry finding.

Quilt batting

The cotton, wool, or polyester "filling" that goes in between the quilt's front and back sections, forming a "quilt sandwich" and adding thickness and warmth.

Resin

A glossy, durable liquid that coats or seals a finished piece. Always work in a well-ventilated space when pouring or curing resin.

Rotary cutter

A small, precise hand tool with a very sharp, round blade attached to a handle, used for cutting fabric, especially along an edge or pattern. It makes cutting straight, accurate lines easy, especially when used with a quilt ruler and **self-healing cutting mat**. Never use a rotary cutter on a bare floor or tabletop.

Royal icing

A meringue-based icing that is ideal for creating detailed decorative effects on cakes. It is pliable when you begin working with it, and hard and specific once it sets. Making royal icing from scratch can be tricky; powdered meringue mixes, available in supermarkets and baking-supply stores, make an easy job of it.

Self-healing cutting mat

Used with a **rotary cutter** or cutting knife, self-healing mats are made of a flexible high-tech plastic that yields to the blade of the knife to help make cut lines clean and straight, then "self-heals," or returns to its flat state for infinitely continued use. These durable mats will protect your work surface and come in many sizes.

Transfer pen or pencil

A special pen or pencil for drawing or tracing an embroidery or other decorative pattern onto paper and then transferring to fabric by applying a hot iron to the back of the paper.

Weaving in ends

To hide the loose strands of yarn left on a finished knitting project, you "weave in": thread a loose end onto a yarn needle, then weave it into your knitting securely, matching the grain of the knitting, and snip the end. Repeat to tuck away all loose strands.

Whipstitch

A simple hand-sewing technique used to join two pieces, or close an opening, securely.

Wool roving

Combed wool ready to be spun or needle-felted, in natural (undyed) state or a variety of colors.

Worsted-weight yarn

A light- to medium-weight general-purpose yarn for knitting or crocheting, designated a 4 in the CYCA system.

X-acto knife

A sharp and precise light-duty cutting instrument ideal for general craft projects.

Yarn needle

A big-eyed, blunt-tipped needle ideal for weaving yarn ends into a finished knitted or crocheted piece.

Zigzag stitch

A sewing machine stitch ideal for joining fabric as well as appliquéing or edging a design, especially with a narrow, tight setting.

RESOURCES

TECHNIQUES AND SUPPLIES

Support your local craft store—you can often find everything from magnetic sheets and glue to felt and jewelry findings there. Art supply stores have many things you'll need for projects like these; I found my foam core sheets, paint, and colored paper at mine. Pick up tools and materials like sandpaper, super-fine steel wool, and primer at your local hardware store, and browse well-stocked fabric stores for thread, buttons, trims, batting, and other quilting needs. Aquarium or gardening shops should set you up nicely for terrarium making, and specialty stores like jewelry-making and beading boutiques and knitting shops are perfect for finding just the right thing to embellish your project, too.

I recommend these wonderful books, resources and Web sites for more help with your craft projects!

Appliqué
Appliqué Your Way and *Complete Embellishing* by Kayte Terry

Beading and jewelry making
Bead Simple by Susan Beal
Naughty Secretary Club: Jewelry for the Working Girl by Jennifer Perkins
Beadsimple.com
Firemountaingems.com
Riogrande.com

Cakes
Bakeitpretty.com
Cakecentral.com

Costuming
Alleycatscratch.com
Costumersguide.com

Crochet
Crochet Adorned by Linda Permann
Ravelry.com

Cross-stitch
Subversive Cross-Stitch by Julie Jackson
Pcstitch.com
Spriters-resource.com
Subversivecrossstitch.com

Decals
Beldecal.com
Lazertran.com

Embroidery
Sublime Stitching and *Embroidered Effects* by Jenny Hart
Sublimestitching.com

Fuse beads
Hamabeads.com
Koolstuff4kids.com
Pcstitch.com

Knitting
Stitch & Bitch by Debbie Stoller
Ravelry.com

LED crafts
Fashion Geek: Clothes Accessories Tech by Diana Eng
Arduino.cc
Evilmadscientist.com
Makershed.com

Needle-felting
Feltique by Nikola Davidson and Brookelynn Morris
Homeecshop.com
Urbanfaunastudio.com

Paper mosaic
Perfect Paper Mosaics by Susan Seymour
Mosaic-tile-guide.com

Printing and stenciling
Bend the Rules with Fabric by Amy Karol
Lotta Prints by Lotta Jansdotter
Utrecht.com

Quilting

Denyse Schmidt Quilts by Denyse Schmidt
Modern Quilt Workshop by Weeks Ringle and Bill Kerr
Purlsoho.com

Sewing

Bend-the-Rules Sewing by Amy Karol
Reader's Digest Guide to Sewing
Sew Darn Cute by Jenny Ryan
Fabricdepot.com
Fabricshoppersunite.com
Rosecitytextiles.com

Terrariums

The New Terrarium by Tovah Martin
Ikea.com (great for inexpensive jars of all sizes)

GEEKERY ONLINE

Boingboing.net

A lavishly updated stream of posts about science, design, technology, inventions, curiosities and everything in between.

Evilmadscientist.com

An inspiring blog and forum, an inviting shop, and home to the Great Internet Migratory Box of Electronics Junk (among many other magnificent things).

Geekologie.com

Trekkie cocktails, gadgets and gizmos reviews, and everything in between.

Homesciencetools.com

Offers a great selection of science teaching kits, which can be cannibalized for all kinds of crafty uses. They also sell very reasonably priced microscope slides.

Lego.com

You can buy any LEGO brick or figure individually here, mixing and matching them to your special craft project.

Makershed.com

Originally launched as a source for back issues of *MAKE:* magazine, the Maker Shed is the online store for CRAFT: and MAKE: project kits, supplies, back issues, books, and so many other cool things. See makezine.com, craftzine.com.

Makezine.com

Find both the *MAKE:* print magazine and its glorious offshoot blog here. Projects, columns, inspiring bits and pieces—this is LED heaven.

NASA

Look for the fantastic and copyright-free image gallery at nasa. gov/multimedia/imagegallery/

Popsci.com

The *Popular Science* online magazine features current issues as well their entire 137-year archive for free browsing. See the DIY section for geekcraft potential galore.

Starwars.com

Visit the spectacular universe of *Star Wars* books and projects, and get a peek at life inside Lucasfilm.

Thinkgeek.com

Find your geeky T-shirts, gizmos, caffeine, and tchotchkes here.

Wired.com

Engaging articles on science, sci-fi, gadgets, and geek culture for all ends of the spectrum.

CRAFTINESS ONLINE

Burdastyle.com

A diverse open-source sewing and pattern-making community.

Craftster.org

A wonderfully massive forum covering all things crafty: swaps, meet-ups, how-tos, crafty questions, and everything in between.

Craftstylish.com
A collection of great craft projects to try, from sewing and knitting to embroidery and beadwork, contributed by dozens of designers.

Craftzine.com
Sister site to *MAKE*: magazine and the epicenter of modern crafting, with original tutorials, reposts of great projects from elsewhere, and lots of advice.

eBay.com
Find everything from Princess Leia action figures to vintage sci-fi books and film stills at this mega-auction site.

Etsy.com
Admire, sell, or buy crafts (or vintage or new supplies) at this huge online marketplace of the handmade.

Getcrafty.com
One of the first crafty sites on the Internet.

Ravelry.com
A resource and forum for all things knitting, crochet, and yarn related.

Supernaturale.com
Front-page articles and links on all things crafty, along with a lively community posting about projects and giving and receiving crafty advice on the forums.

Thistothat.com
If you're gluing strange things to other strange things, this Web site will tell you the right kind of glue to use.

GEEKCRAFT (AND BEYOND) ONLINE

Flickr.com
A huge photo-sharing site with themed groups including some amazing geeky craft collections, from Coraline box mystery swaps to video-game needlework.

Geekcrafts.com
A daily blog of all things geeky and crafty—submit your own creation or send in one you've fallen for!

Instructables.com
A huge archive of step-by-step video tutorials for making all kinds of things.

Spritestitch.com
A fantastic video-game craft blog and forum with plenty of projects to try.

Starwars.com/kids
Pull down the Kids menu and click on Crafts to enter Bonnie Burton's super-inspiring Star Wars Kids Crafts archive inside Starwars.com.

WoW.com
The World of Warcrafts online community contains a staggering array of craft projects, impressively curated. Search for individual projects by name or genre, or check out the whole archive at Wow.com/category/world-of-warcrafts.

ACKNOWLEDGMENTS

First, thank you so much to my talented project contributors: geekcrafters extraordinaire Shelbi Roach, Garth Johnson, Heather Mann, John Lohman (times two!), Ryan and Lucy Berkley, Cathy Pitters, Linda Permann, Diane Gilleland, Lee Meredith, Erika Kern, Rachel Hobson, Joshua and Sarah Moon, Shayne Rioux, Paul Overton, Julie Ramsey, Ruth Suehle (also times two!), Adaiha Covington, and Kayte Terry and Adam Louie.

A heartfelt thank-you to my brilliant writers, who illuminated so many fascinating facets of geek culture: Vincent Morrison, Bonnie Burton, Chelsea Cain, Renee Asher, Kim Mohan, Ruth Suehle, Katin Imes, and Pete Bejarano.

Thank you to my generous and helpful friends who shared their talents in so many other ways! Daniela Caine, my Harry Potter robe pattern tester (who sewed the toddler size so beautifully); Ryan Myers Tinsel, for expert basement d20 drilling; Amy Corcoran, for a lovely Coraline box consultation; Chelsea, my D&D muse; Ruth, who imparted her impressively varied geeky expertise throughout; Bonnie, who has the coolest job in the world; Shayne, for inviting me to be part of geekcrafts with her and Renee; and my nephew, Julian Quaresima, for sharing the secrets of all his favorite Wii games. Thank you so much to Diane and to Tina Barseghian for encouraging me to write the book in the first place, and to Natalie Zee Drieu for her kind support as well. And thank you to Lisa Poisso and everyone at World of WarCrafts for your help choosing just the right WoW craft for the collection!

Thank you to my wonderful editors, Jodi Warshaw and Laura Lee Mattingly, for partnering with me on this fantastic and very fun project, and thank you as always to my stellar agent, Stacey Glick. Thank you to to Alexis Hartman for the beautiful, precise how-to illustrations and pattern templates she created; to Jay B Sauceda for the amazing photographs; and to Will Bryant for the awesome hand drawings.

A huge thank-you to my amazing husband, Andrew. I am so fortunate to have you as my partner in life and crafts alike. And of course to my daughter, Pearl, who inspires, entertains, and fascinates me every day . . . and lets me make her the geeky Halloween costumes of my dreams. I can't wait to read the Harry Potter books and watch the *Star Wars* movies with you.

And speaking of *Star Wars* . . . thank you to my dad for taking me to see *The Empire Strikes Back* and introducing me to this whole world.

The members of Public School would like to thank: Jessica Olsen for asistance and production, Eric from Wonko's (Cylon Centurion figure), Nicole McGarry of Wicked Cakes (LilyPad Cake), and all other Public School members for being patient with the cover photo shoot being in the lounge, and last but not least, Andrew "Velocischapter" Schapiro for his tireless efforts and uncanny wit.

INDEX

POW! ZAP! MAGNETS

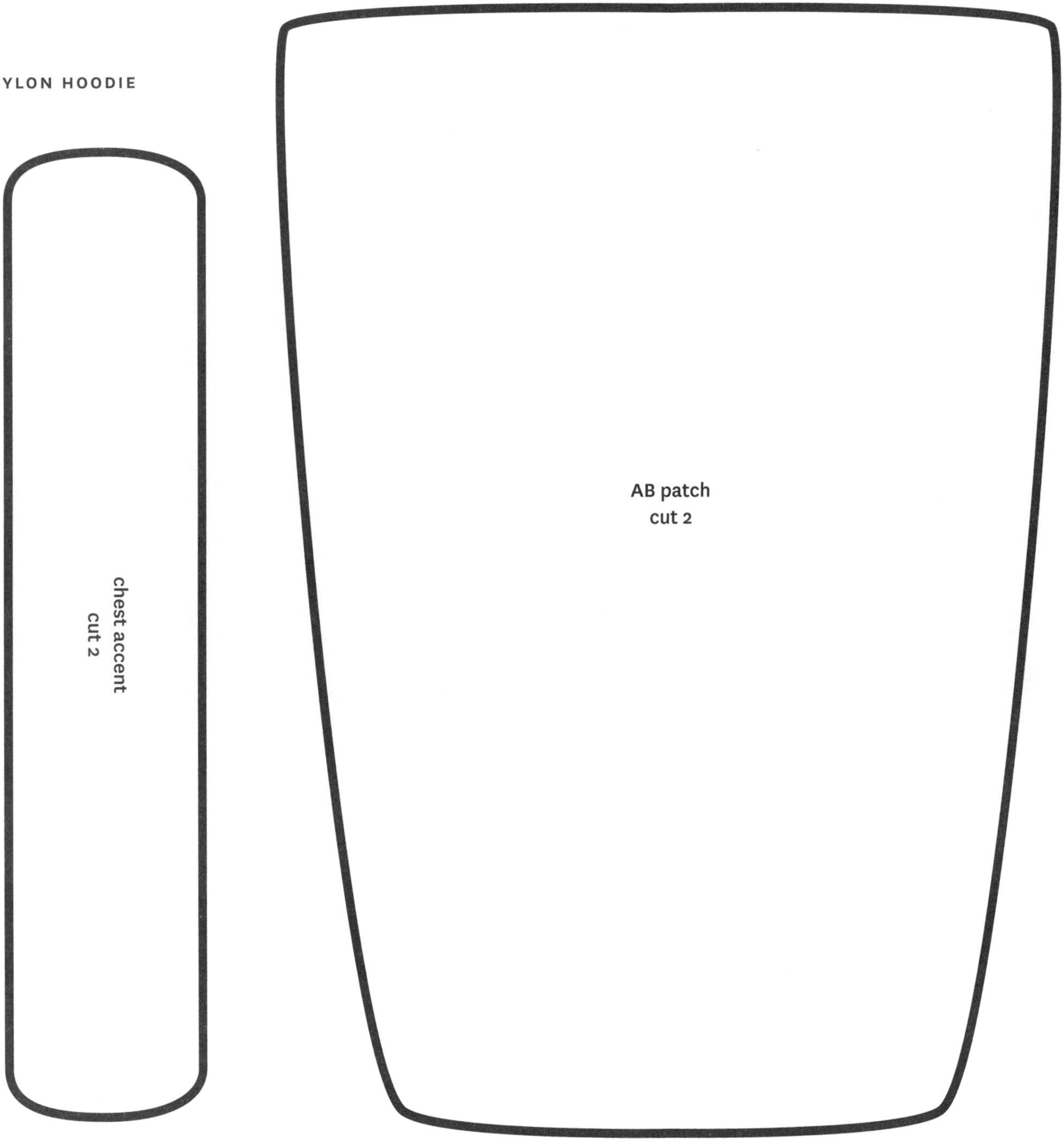

CYLON HOODIE

chest accent
cut 2

AB patch
cut 2

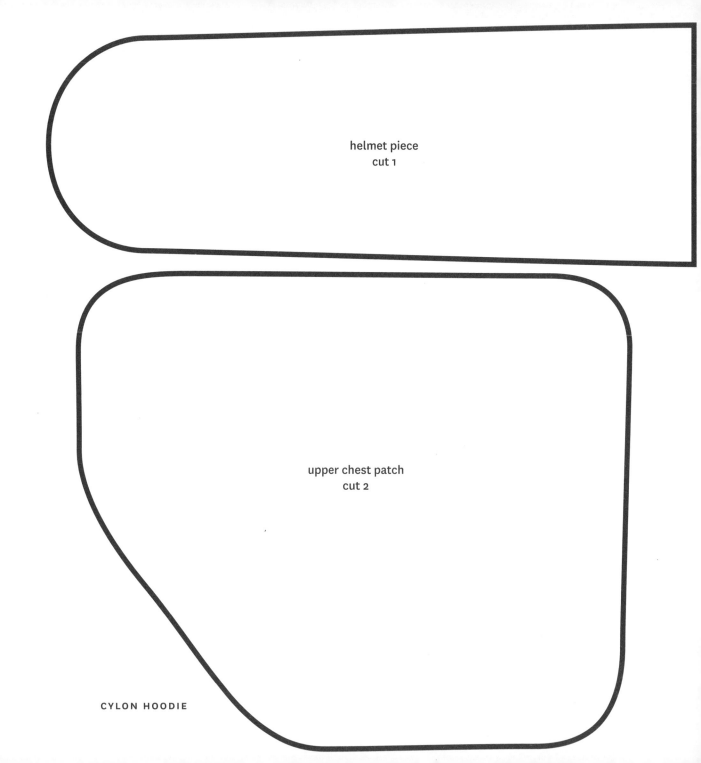

helmet piece
cut 1

upper chest patch
cut 2

CYLON HOODIE

fold

back panel
cut 1

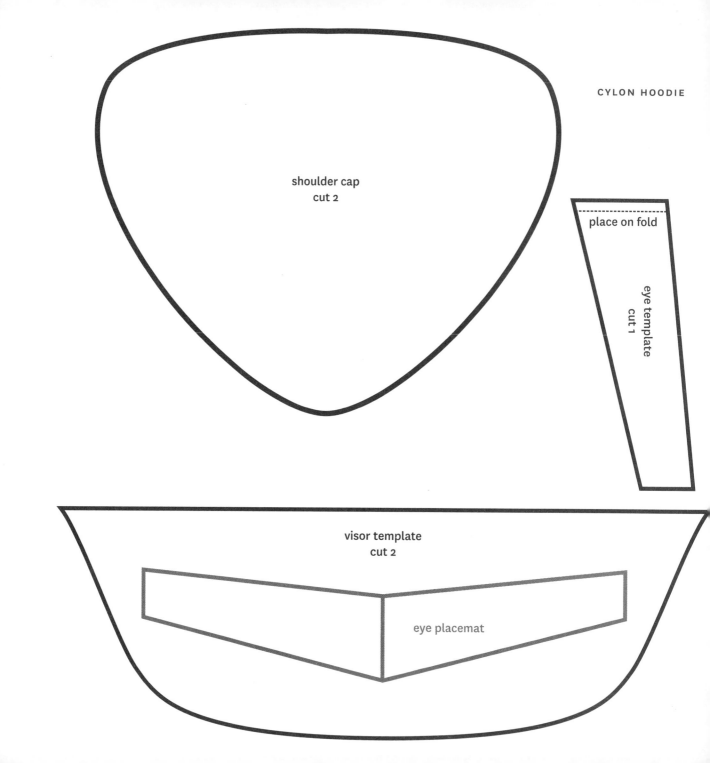

CYLON HOODIE

shoulder cap
cut 2

place on fold

eye template
cut 1

visor template
cut 2

eye placemat

STAR WARS TERRARIUMS

LOST SWAN STATION LOGBOOK COVER
Enlarge 20%

DI: 4815162342

HOT CHOCOLATE
POWDER MIX

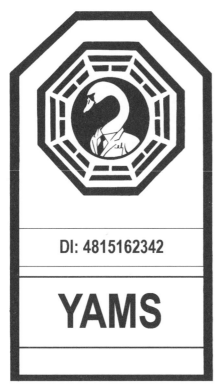

LOST YAMS LABEL

LOST PEAS LABEL

9210408:28	accepted	9210410:16	accepted	9220412:04
accepted	922041:52	accepted	922043:40	accepted
922045:28	accepted	922047:16	accepted	922049:04
accepted	9220410:52	accepted	9220412:40	accepted
922042:28	accepted	922044:16	SYSTEM	FAILURE
SYSTEM	FAILURE	SYSTEM	FAILURE	SYSTEM
SYSTEM	FAILURE	SYSTEM	FAILURE	SYSTEM
SYSTEM	FAILURE	SYSTEM	FAILURE	SYSTEM
SYSTEM	FAILURE	SYSTEM	FAILURE	SYSTEM
SYSTEM	FAILURE	SYSTEM	FAILURE	SYSTEM
SYSTEM	FAILURE	SYSTEM	FAILURE	SYSTEM
SYSTEM	FAILURE	SYSTEM	FAILURE	SYSTEM
SYSTEM	FAILURE	SYSTEM	FAILURE	SYSTEM
SYSTEM	FAILURE	SYSTEM	FAILURE	SYSTEM
SYSTEM	FAILURE	SYSTEM	FAILURE	SYSTEM
SYSTEM	FAILURE	SYSTEM	FAILURE	SYSTEM
SYSTEM	FAILURE	SYSTEM	FAILURE	SYSTEM
SYSTEM	FAILURE	SYSTEM	FAILURE	SYSTEM
SYSTEM	FAILURE	SYSTEM	FAILURE	SYSTEM
SYSTEM	FAILURE	SYSTEM	FAILURE	SYSTEM
SYSTEM	FAILURE	SYSTEM	FAILURE	SYSTEM
SYSTEM	FAILURE	SYSTEM	FAILURE	SYSTEM

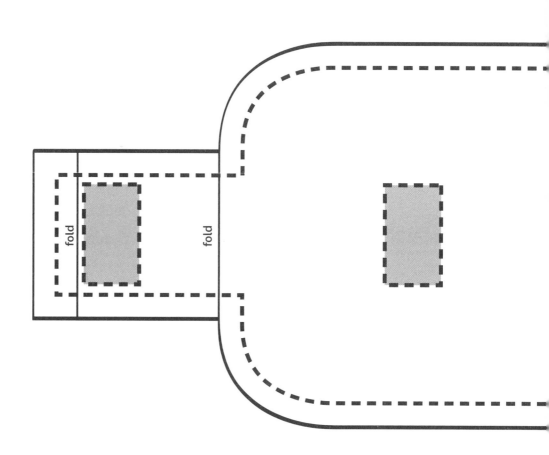

fold

fold

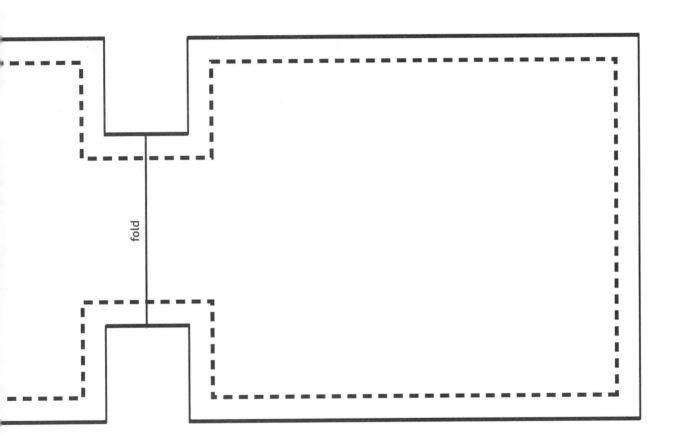

fold

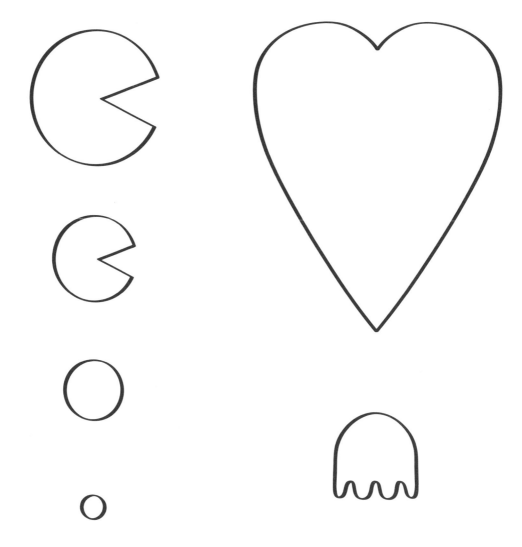

36

Kr

Krypton
83.80

99

Es

Einsteinium
[252]

14

Si

Silicon
28.086

elastic loop

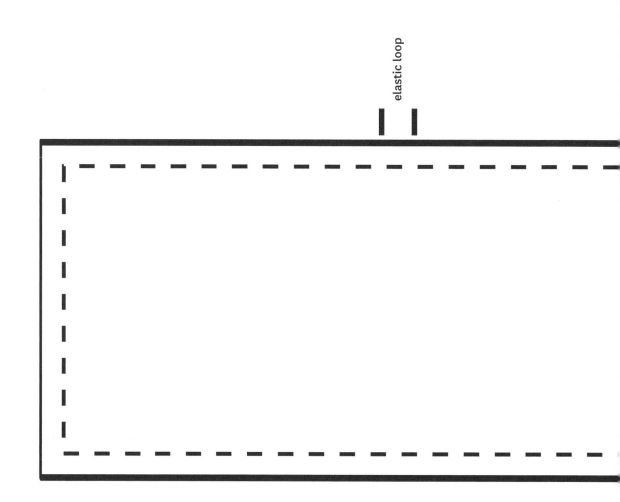

HARRY POTTER INSIGNIA

leave open

yarn

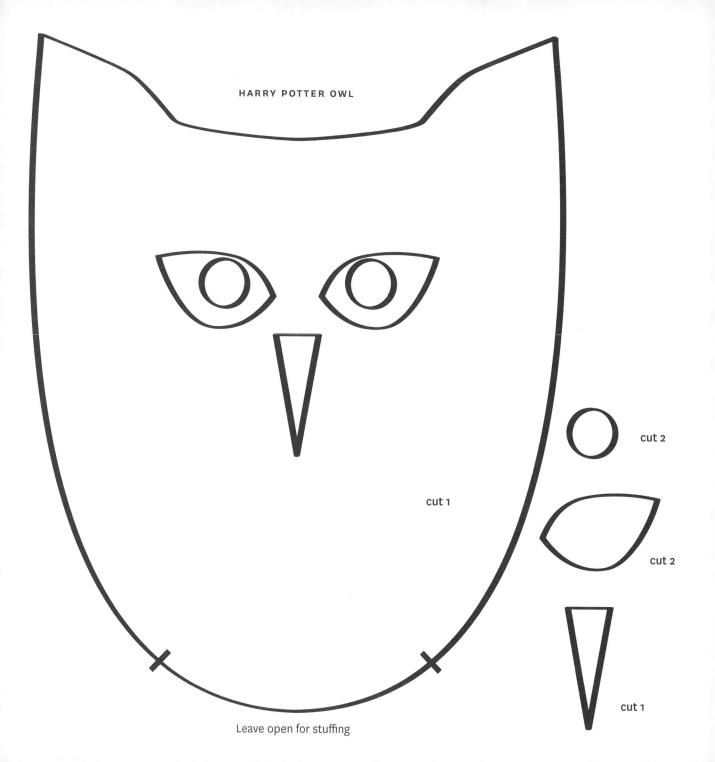

HARRY POTTER OWL

cut 2

cut 1

cut 2

cut 1

Leave open for stuffing

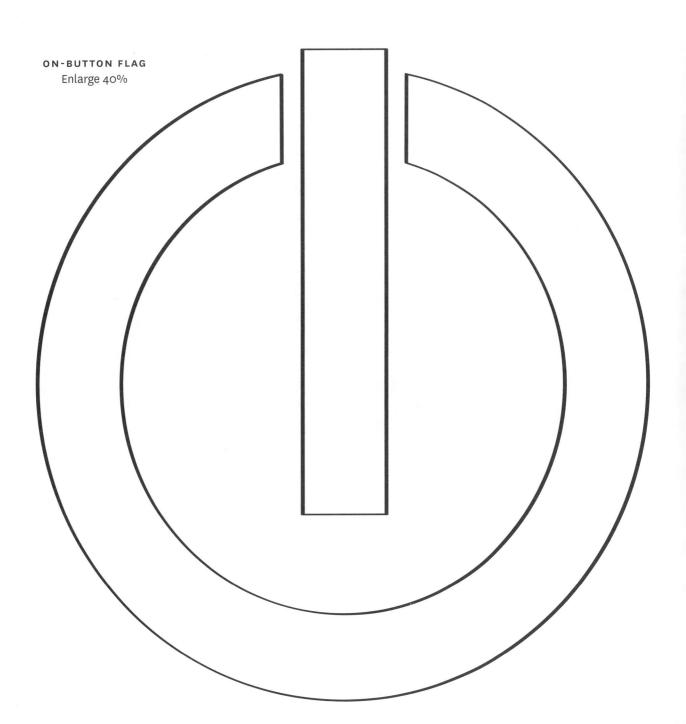

ON-BUTTON FLAG
Enlarge 40%

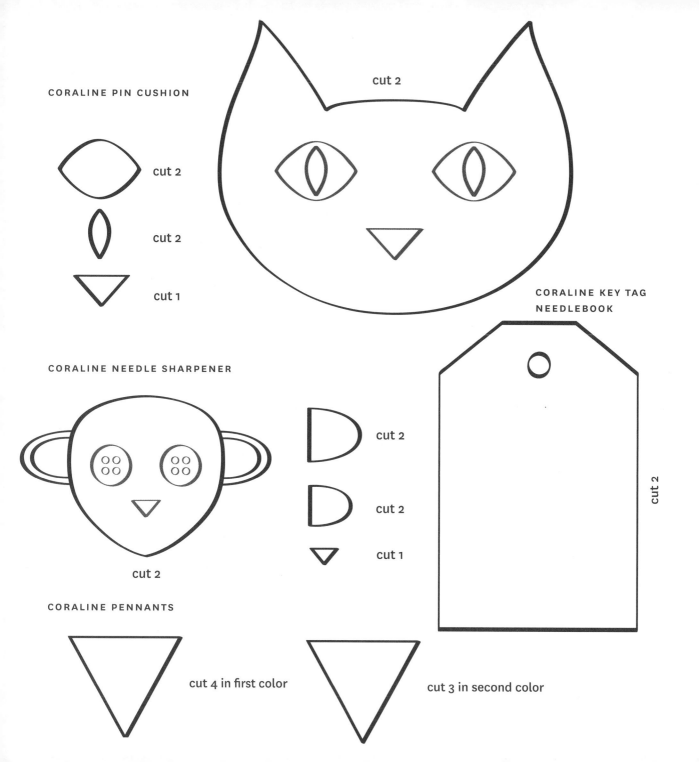

CORALINE PIN CUSHION

cut 2

cut 2

cut 1

cut 2

CORALINE KEY TAG
NEEDLEBOOK

cut 2

CORALINE NEEDLE SHARPENER

cut 2

cut 2

cut 1

cut 2

CORALINE PENNANTS

cut 4 in first color

cut 3 in second color

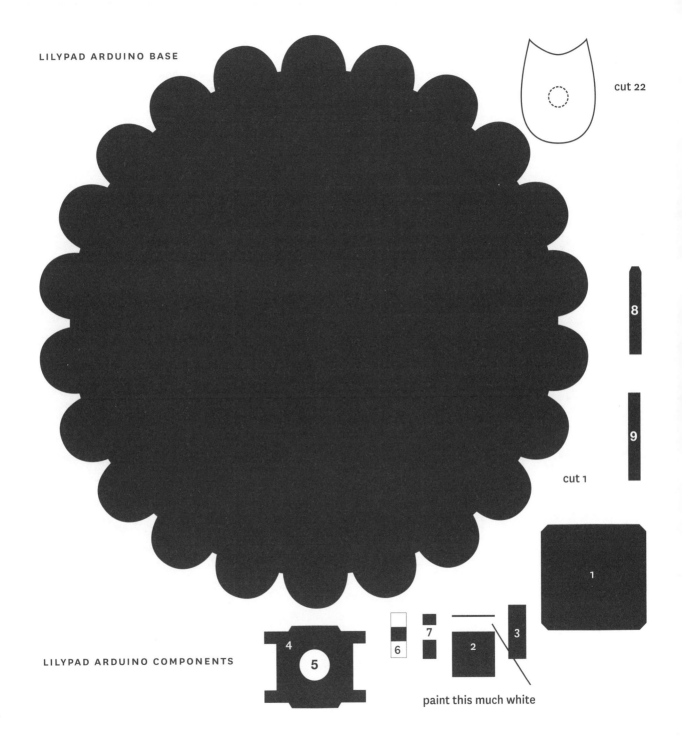

LILYPAD ARDUINO BASE

cut 22

cut 1

8

9

1

LILYPAD ARDUINO COMPONENTS

4

5

6

7

2

3

paint this much white

VINTAGE SCI-FI BOOK COZY
Enlarge 10%

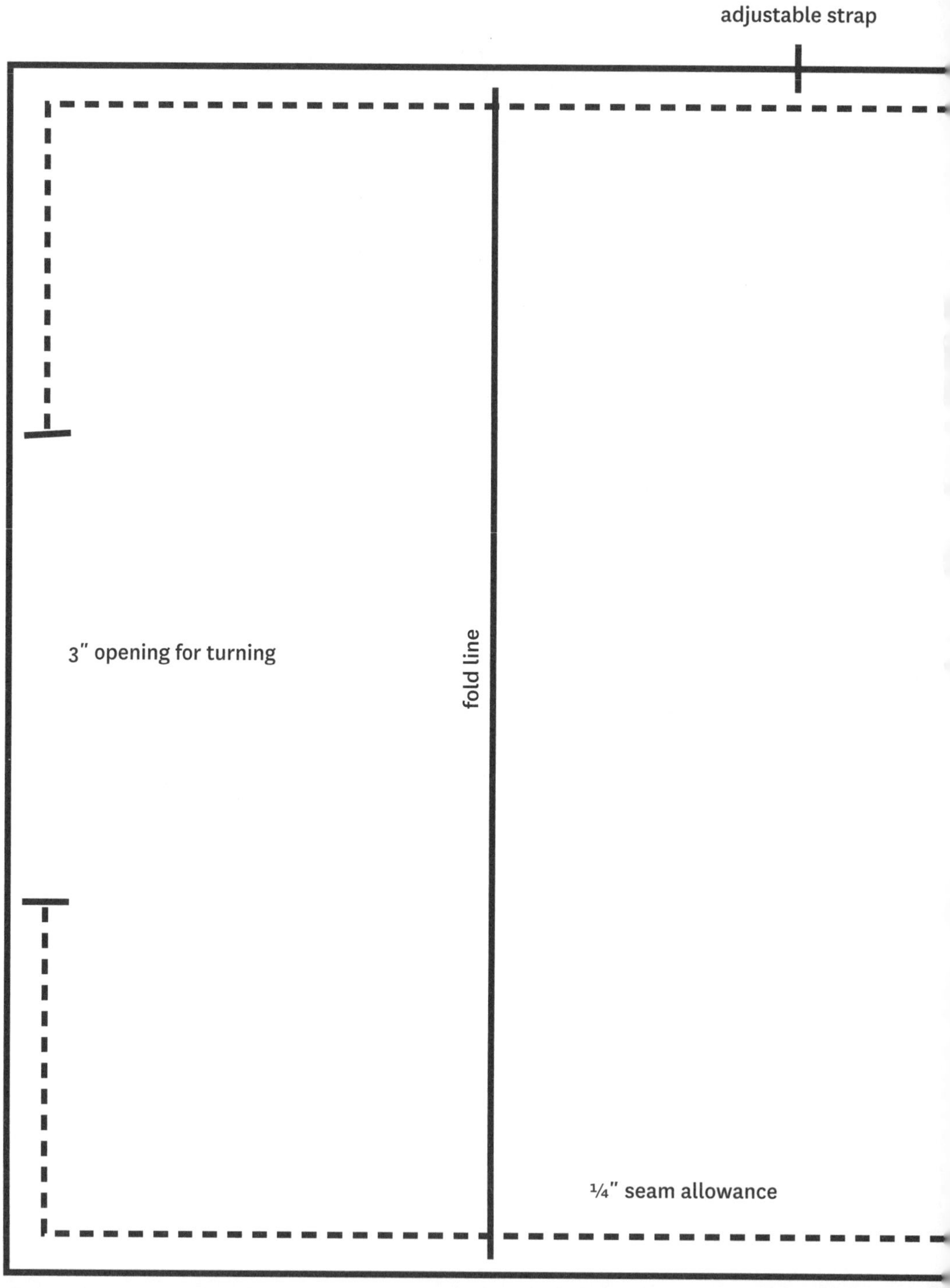
adjustable strap
3″ opening for turning
fold line
¼″ seam allowance

bookmark placement

fold line

fold line

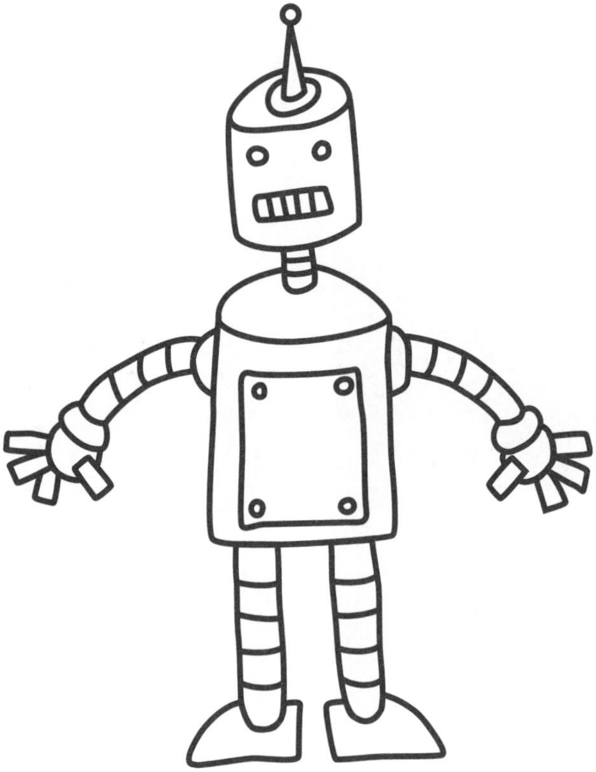

fold line

ROBOT STENCIL

ROBOT EMBROIDERY

ER-GEEK-ONOMIC WOODEN MOUSE PAD

DRIVE-IN MESSENGER BAG
Enlarge 60%

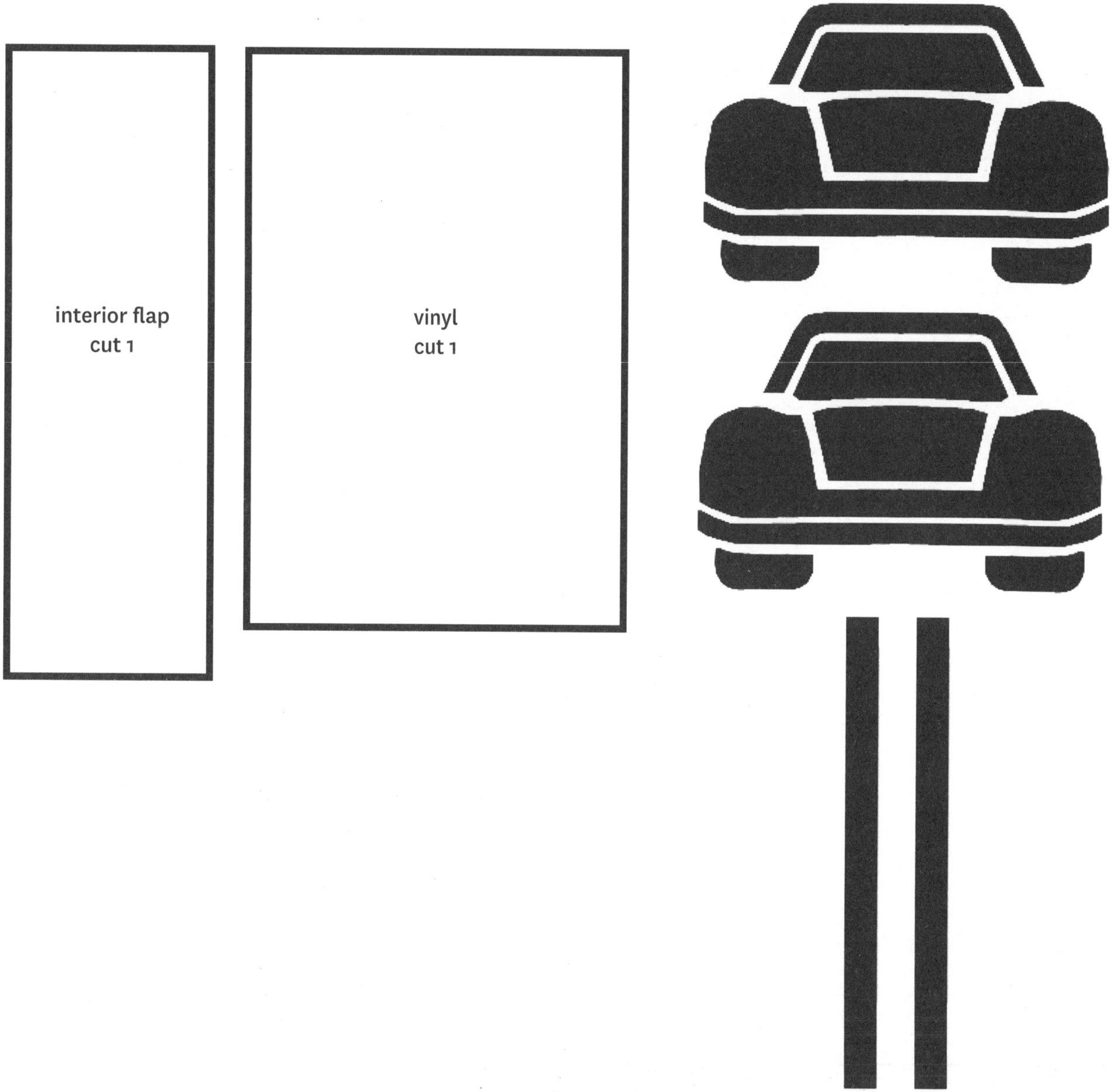

interior flap
cut 1

vinyl
cut 1